Joyce Storey was born in Kingswood, near Bristol, in 1917. After leaving school at the age of 14 she worked in service for a brief period before starting a seven-year stint, working in a corset factory. On the eve of the Second World War she married John Storey, an airforce man, with whom she had three daughters and a son. In 1983, at age 66, frustrated by what life seemed to offer her, Joyce joined the Bristol Broadsides writer's work-shop and began her autobiography.

Joyce Storey, now retired, and partially sighted, still lives in Bristol. She has five grandchildren and a great-granddaughter, and is currently working on the third volume of her autobiography. Virago also publish *Our Joyce*, the story of her early years.

Joyce's War

1939 – 1945

Joyce Storey

Published by VIRAGO PRESS Limited, 1992
20–23 Mandela Street, Camden Town, London NW1 0HQ

Copyright © Joyce Storey, 1990

First published in Britain by Bristol Broadsides, 1990

The right of Joyce Storey to be identified as the author of this
work has been asserted by her in accordance with the Copyright,
Designs and Patents Act 1988

A CIP catalogue record for this book is available from the British Library

Printed in Britain by Cox and Wyman Ltd, Reading, Berks

My grateful thanks to my daughter Pat, who gave so much of her precious time to correct this manuscript and to steer me through the clumsy bits.

To my life long friend, Vee, who shared and enthused about every completed chapter. Her words, 'I'm proud of my mate', were the boost and the spur. We shared our secrets as children and it seems right that she share my book.

Finally, I take this space and opportunity to thank all the many readers who wrote expressing their pleasure after reading *Our Joyce*. It was their warmth and enthusiasm that inspired me to write this sequel. *Joyce's War* deals with the war and the early years of my marriage. Many of my older readers may have had similar experiences and will be able to relate to mine.

This book is dedicated to my best friend Vee's daughter Ann, and to my own daughters Pat and Jacky.

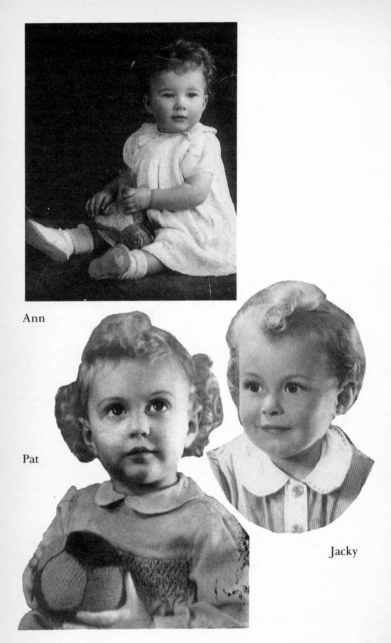

Ann

Pat

Jacky

Preface

In 1939, two momentous things happened. The first was my marriage to Bertie Storey, a childhood admirer. This happened on a very hot day, July 23rd, which was my twenty-second birthday and another good reason why I shall never forget it. The second staggering event of that year was the outbreak of war on Sunday September 3rd, just six short weeks after my marriage. The shock waves of that war had such far-reaching effects that the people of my generation never quite recovered from it.

I viewed both events with mixed feelings. Born at the end of the Great War in 1917, I grew up with all the horrific stories still so fresh in the minds of my parents and the people of their generation — the appalling conditions in the trenches; the policy of attrition which was so desperately costly with the deaths of all those young men; the gassing and the shellshock and the misery of all those broken lives. It seemed to us that this cruel, senseless war impoverished England, and it was portrayed through our schooldays in such a way that the Germans, with their funny spiked helmets, struck terror in our minds and hatred in our hearts. That was to have been The War to End All Wars, and it was unthinkable, throughout the later years of the 1930s, that we were on the brink of another. As for my marriage, I was both apprehensive, and desperate for it to succeed. In a strange kind of way, by making a success of my marriage, I felt I could prove something to my mother. Her unhappy relationship with my father and my own severed bond with her filled me with a deep sense of guilt which I could not shake off. I knew I was being drawn into a similar set of circumstances, yet having to prove that this need not be so. So all my effort would be for her and not for me; I carried this great burden all my life.

All that long, hot, lush summer, Bertie pursued me

and pressured me. He was in the Royal Air Force and due to fly out to his next posting in Ceylon. He painted a rosy picture of how my life would be as his wife. I daydreamed of sun-drenched beaches, of warm tropical seas and clear blue skies; of hours of pleasant idleness as I lay in the sun and became a bronzed goddess. I was carried along on the bubble of his dream. Alas, I sold my freedom and independence for a mirage.

1 · *From Miss to Mrs*

No hint of any shock waves about to be unleashed came
to us as we stepped from the cool interior of the church
out into the blazing sunshine of that July day, and walked
the short distance along the path to the little wicket gate
that brought us out into the Kingswood High Street
again. I remember we waited for a tram car that would
take Bertie on the first stage of his journey back to
Calshot, where he was based. He had been given a 24
hour pass to get wed by Special Licence and was already
two hours overdue. We learned later that on his return
he had been put on jankers, RAF jargon for punishment
duties. We often laughed about how he spent his wedding night spud bashing.

After I had waved him goodbye, I stood for a long time
contemplating the short time it had taken to get 'catched'.
All that spring and summer, the whole of Kingswood,
including the corset factory where I worked, had been
caught up in frenzied marriage fever, as though Nature
was insisting that we pair off to ensure the survival of the
species. I too had been caught up in that fever, but felt
more like a victim than a prize, all my logic telling me that
this move was not right for me, and to resist it at all costs.
The love dust that dreams are made of and poets rave
about must have dulled my senses and, like a reluctant
mallard duckling on the pond of life, I was rounded up
for Nature to take its course and set me in my place.
Reluctance and rebellion have no place in the natural
scheme of things.

I looked down at the ring on my finger and realised
what I had done. It seemed unfamiliar and irritated me,
so that on impulse I took it off, and when I got home, I
slipped it onto a gold chain and wore it round my neck.

I returned to work, telling no one of my marriage.
Things returned to normal and I even forgot my

1

changed status, and as the time slipped by, I began to think it had all been a dream. This calm was shattered one morning when Charles Ryall came bounding up the packing room stairs two at a time, demanding to know if there was a Mrs Storey in the room. Nobody moved — not even me. That strange, unreal ceremony with no friends there to wish me well or to throw confetti along my path had been pushed into the dark recess of my mind long since. We all stood there like statues, mouthing 'nobody here of that name'. Even the charge hand stood inert with a pair of corsets poised in her hand. As I watched them all shaking their heads, it came to me slowly and painfully that I was the Mrs Storey he was talking about, and with my face reddening I blurted out, 'Please, sir — it's me'.

Charlie Ryall laughed whilst everybody else looked on. Here was gossip that would break the monotony for the rest of the day.

My new status had been needed in the office for working purposes, and I was foolish not to have realised this. But I was still angry because I thought I should have been summoned to the office where I could have been given more privacy about my affairs. After he had clattered back down the steps again, Mr Woolrich, our Manager, told everybody to attend to their work as too much time had already been wasted.

At lunch time I was surrounded by workmates who demanded to know how long I had kept that little secret up my sleeve, and clucked with excitement when I embroidered the whole episode and lied that we had gone away secretly to get wed by Special Licence.

'Not even our parents knew,' I said, and they looked dreamy and sighed and murmured,

'How romantic.'

Gasps of delight went round the room when I produced the ring and murmured,

'Welsh gold.'

When they passed by, they would squeeze my arm and

wish me well. The looks of rapture as they went back to their work showed that they were dreaming that some romance like the one I had so vividly lied about would enrich their own lives. I felt an overwhelming sense of guilt, and wondered what they would say if only they knew that I would willingly have changed back to their single status given less than half a chance.

However, although the flicks were still a weekly pleasure that most of us would not miss for the world, there were disturbing reports about Hitler and his storm troopers parading in Berlin. The voice of Bob Danvers Walker on the Pathe Gazette news worried us a little, but by the time the big film was underway, Hitler and Europe seemed so very far away. In the streets during the next few weeks, we were stopped and asked to sign petitions to say that we did not want a war. We foolishly thought that we had reached the age of reason, that talks round the table were the order of the day, and war was now outdated and uncivilised.

We bought our cheap day rail tickets to the West coast and on Saturdays queued in the hot August sunshine for trips down the river on Campbell's steamer, or we picnicked on the Downs and strolled along to the sea walls to watch the people and the river below. So the days passed, slow and leisurely, and I was as happy as I could be in the circumstances.

Our wireless set sat squarely in the middle of the sideboard in the recess by the side of the fireplace. We had taken down the glass cupboard just above, but had retained two shelves. The lower one now housed a battery and this was what my father was changing when I came into the room on that fateful day.

He had rushed up to the garage to get the recharged battery and was twiddling with the fresh leads along with a mountain of wires that mother was always grumbling about and which he hid from sight by allowing the tangled mass to fall behind the sideboard. Mrs Baker and her daughter, Barbara, were already there, sitting on the

3

sofa. She did not have a wireless set and always came in to us to hear the King's special Christmas message. Mrs Baker was very patriotic and loved tradition, pomp and ceremony. She had sat and cried when Edward VIII abdicated.

There were two large knobs on the wireless, which Dad began to twiddle to bring in the station. There seemed to be a lot of interference and oscillation. In the midst of all this, there was a knock on the front door. My mother went to investigate, calling over her shoulder for Dad to quit mucking about with the 'damn set'. She returned with Elsie, Bert and David Storey from across the road. Elsie was flushed and agitated, and explained hurriedly that Bert had forgotten to put their batteries on charge and now the set was as dead as a Dodo. They had hurried over to us because they knew we wouldn't mind. Elsie hugged me, then we all moved up to make room for them just as the chimes of Big Ben solemnly rang out the hour of eleven. Mrs Saunders, our next door neighbour, poked her head round the door and we all simultaneously hissed,

'Ssshhhhh.'

She sat down obediently on the arm of a chair and kept repeating softly,

'Oh my Gawd, oh my Gawd,' and trying to retrieve hairpins that had slipped from the straggly knotted bun at the nape of her neck, occasionally brushing back wisps of wayward hair from her forehead with the back of her hand.

Everybody listened in silence to the voice of Neville Chamberlain as he began to tell us that Germany had been given until eleven o'clock that morning to withdraw her troops from Poland.

'No such undertaking has been given,' he said. 'So it is with regret that I have to tell you that England is now at war with Germany.'

Mrs Baker cried openly and clung to her daughter, who cried with her. Mrs Saunders again called on the

4

Lord to save us all because she was convinced that they would use poison gas on us this time. Elsie remarked that she had spoken to Mr Fry, the local Councillor and her next-door neighbour, and he had told her in confidence that the first consignment of gas masks due to be delivered the following week would be far from adequate and it was a question of distribution. Whoever got there first would be lucky.

Elsie was right about the gas masks, and several weeks later there was a mad panic for these frightful looking things at local school rooms, where they were being distributed. People reacted in the most uncivilised way because they were so certain that poison gas would be used by the Germans and there were not enough gas masks issued on that first delivery. We carried them everywhere with us. In fact, it became a kind of ritual to say each time we ventured forth,

'Don't forget, Gas Mask, Identity Card and Torch.'

The Identity Cards had to be carried in wallets and handbags at all times. My identity number was TKBR/82/10. There was a brisk trade done with identity bracelets and necklaces. We bought special ones for loved ones and friends. Shelters were erected in back gardens. Ours took up all the small dirt square, with the opening coming right up to the edge of the path. Each street had an Air Raid Warden. My father was the warden for our street. He had no flowers to look at now, but spent hours looking up into the sky.

Towards the middle of September, I received a letter from Bertie, which seemed to be the crowning blow. It briefly stated that all leave had been cancelled, and that the crew of High Speed Launch 111 would be proceeding forthwith to Grimsby, where they would be patrolling the Humber in liaison with the Royal Navy. Bertie was negotiating with Flying Officer Bowen the possibility of obtaining a sleeping-out pass. If this was acquired, then as soon as possible he would find some digs and then send for me. I was to stand by and await instructions.

I had never envisaged for one moment that I would be deprived of my Ceylon trip. It never occurred to me that even a war would prevent us from taking the journey to another place and a new life. The whole reason for saying yes to Bertie was on account of the glowing picture he painted of how our life could be in that warm and delightful place. I had made the supreme sacrifice for nothing.

Grimsby — where on earth was Grimsby? As far as I knew, it was somewhere 'up North', on the cold East Coast. I'd dreamed of tropical beaches, the warmth of golden sun, now all I was going to get was the cold grey North Sea and bitter winds. I felt angry and frustrated.

'I might just as well stay here and earn myself some money. That way I might get the deposit for a house,' I said angrily to my mother.

To my surprise, she told me rather sharply that I could forget that idea right away.

'Your place is where your husband wants you to be. You made your bed my girl, so now you go and lie on it.'

She then implied that she also was entitled to a life of her own and that she and Dad were thinking of moving, buying a little business of their own. Now that I was married, it would be my husband's responsibility to find me a home. I could no longer regard South Road as that.

'Come upstairs, I have something for you. It's a present from me and Dad.'

She knew that her words about South Road never being my home again had sobered me so that I was crestfallen and sad, but I followed her up the stairs and into the small whitewashed back room where, by the side of the single iron bed, was a neat little brown tin trunk that she confided to me was her only possession on the day that she had left her home at St George to start her new life at South Road. Inside the trunk was a pair of new white wool blankets with blue borders.

In that cold little room, the only splash of colour was the crochet worked squares on the bed cover and, as I

6

stood there, I remember feeling just as bereft and inadequate as the day I had left school. I had but two gifts to start me on my way, the woollen blankets from my Mum and Dad, and a half tea service from Elsie and Bert. It was in a beautiful orange colour. Because I was afraid that I might break it if it was packed and taken with me, I asked Mum if I could leave it behind in the glass cupboard downstairs and collect it later. Perhaps it was just as well that I had no way of knowing then that it would be nine years before I had a real home of my own.

The letter from Bertie finally arrived. He wrote to say that he had found some nice digs and enclosed a railway ticket made out for Grimsby Docks. He emphasised that I must be sure to get off the train at Grimsby Docks, (not Grimsby Town) where he would be waiting to meet me. The tin trunk was carried down the stairs, where I packed the rest of my things that I would need. When it was carefully locked and strapped, I sent it via the railway carrier to my new address at Grimsby Docks Station where Bertie would collect it and make sure it was delivered safely. My transition from maid to married woman had begun.

2 · *A Train Journey*

The sun was quite warm after the early morning mist had cleared, when I left home that dull November day. I wore a fuchsia coloured blouse that went well with my dark hair. I carried my short coat together with the blue velvet holdall that my mother had first made for me when I went away from home at fourteen to my job in service to Mr and Mrs Collins. I was thinking of that episode as I grasped the tortoise shell handles of the bag, amazed at the service it had given me. I had gone from my home then with anxious fears. That venture had ended in disaster. Some good had followed, and the corset factory had given me seven years of good employment, plus a lot of happy memories and friends. Now I was setting off on perhaps the biggest venture of my life. I did not know what lay ahead, but with youthful optimism I reasoned that if as a child I could stand up to my grandfather who was six foot tall, then I could face any challenge that the future might bring. Fortified with this new-found strength, I caught the train for Paddington and watched the countryside speed by.

At Paddington, I extravagantly hailed a taxi to get me across to Kings Cross Station, then sat stiff and tense as we wended our snail like way through the traffic, with the cabby clock ticking up the fare alarmingly. Finally arriving at Kings Cross, I gave the taxi driver the exact fare that he asked me for, and was horrified when he let rip a whole strip of abuse at me. Some of the expletives were very colourful indeed. Never having ridden in a taxi before, I was totally unaware that I was expected to give a tip. Confused and embarrassed, I ran red-faced and scared into the station, and got into the first train I saw. I sat trembling in the corner of the compartment, not daring to move, and not caring if it was the right train or not, till the thudding of my heart and the trembling of my legs had stopped. I finally found courage to put my head out of the window and timidly ask a porter, who was passing hurriedly by, if I was on the right train for Grimsby.

'Change at Peterborough,' was the curt reply.

The huge clock on the station platform pointed giant hands to 2:45. As I sat staring at it, I could actually see the long, pointed minute hand ticking off the seconds. I wondered when the train was due out, but after my experience with the big bad world of taxi drivers, I was glad to settle back into the corner of the train and observe the activity outside from the safety within. I suddenly remembered the tiny flask of tea I had packed and was glad of the stimulus that the drink afforded. I even had

8

time to eat the ham roll carefully packed into my blue velvet holdall. After that, I stood up, brushed the crumbs from my skirt and was about to open the window to enquire about the departure time, when the train gave a sudden gentle jolt as the brakes were released, and this great London Midland & Scottish monster slid slowly out of the station, not gathering speed until we were clear of the maze of streets and rows of backyards and houses; grinding over points, waiting for go-ahead signals, groaning until its giant heart was released and we leapt forward, speeding away out into the countryside with fields and trees and cows and sheep all flashing past. My great adventure had truly begun. As there was no-one in my carriage, I took off my shoes and stretched myself along the length of the seat. The rhythm of the train seemed to be saying, 'I'm taking you to Grimsby. I'm taking you to Grimsby.'

At Peterborough I alighted stiff and cold. I noticed the change in temperature straight away, it must have been several degrees colder. I put on my coat shivering slightly and hurried up the steps to cross to another platform. There was an hour to kill before I could make the final lap of my journey. I would try to get a cup of tea or find the waiting room. The fire in the waiting room was about as low as my spirits — dusk at Peterborough station on that cold November night was far from being warm and friendly. Small knots of people were walking up and down to keep warm and relieve boredom and stiffness. A cigarette would suddenly glow in the half light. Nobody spoke, and on the draughty station the cold night air crept along the walls and along the ground, chilling everything, including the huddled figures standing waiting there.

When the train finally rumbled into view, it was evident that it was already full. The waiting crowd surged forward as it snaked its full length along the platform and I found myself being pushed and jostled. I thought at one point I might get crushed and this might well have

9

happened but for the timely intervention of a soldier opening a door and heaving me easily into the carriage, then moving up on his seat to make room for me. Inside it was warm and I settled back and tried to relax. This was the first time I had had travelling companions and I was relieved. This was obviously a troop train taking the soldiers to various postings in the North and presently they began to take down kitbags and to rummage through for food and chocolate. Flasks and cups appeared from the depths of greatcoats like magic and I was handed a cup of hot cocoa, which I accepted gratefully. After that, talk came easily, and I found myself enjoying the company and joining in the easy flow of conversation. The joking and banter about their enforced new life in strange surroundings made me laugh. Their willingness to adapt to a new situation brought home to me the need to strike a new balance. As I glanced round at all their cheerful faces, I felt a slight envy for the friendships that would be made with all these soldiers thrown together in a common cause. I found myself missing the happy chatter of the girls from the packing department. From now on, I would be on my own in a strange town.

As we neared our destination, the lively communication between us changed to soft whispers. Some of the soldiers slept, their chins deep in khaki greatcoats. I asked the time and was surprised to find that it was 10:30 pm. Just outside the Dock area, there seemed an almost interminable wait — either for the green signal to proceed, or, as it seemed to me, sheer reluctance on the part of the train to go any further. It seemed ages before we limped very slowly into the station and the brakes were applied so sharply that we were almost thrown from our seats.

The same young soldier who had helped me into the carriage at Peterborough now handed me my case from the rack and opened the door, which blew a blast of freezing air into the compartment. He hesitated for a moment, looked along the dark, deserted platform, then

10

said he would make sure I met up with my husband. I turned to wish the now silent companions of my journey goodnight, but they barely moved from their slumbering positions. We heard the hiss of steam from the engine indicating that the train would not linger long, and then we noticed a solitary figure standing hunched and chilled under the one and only dim lamp on the platform. Excitement filled me now; soon I would be feeling warm arms around me. I would be reassured, and everything would be alright again. The soldier and I ran along the platform together. The figure moved in the faint fog of that November night and stepped forward to take the case roughly from the soldier's hand, without so much as a word of thanks to him for his help and solicitude, and began to hustle me away. The soldier was quickly swallowed up in the darkness of the night. He had raced back to the open carriage, and the train was already moving forward as we turned aside to surrender my ticket and walk out of the station on our way to my new home. I sensed that Bertie was jealous when he had seen me with the young man. I knew, too, that I had made a wrong move and a bad impression. I was not elated that my husband was jealous, merely hurt and lost. Confused emotions covered me. I was reminded vividly of another desolate moment, oh so long ago. I followed him silently out of the station. We did not speak. There was nothing to say.

3 · *Wrong Beginning*

A row of red brick three storey houses faced an embankment on top of which coal trucks rumbled monotonously and incessantly all day long. These slow-moving tubs of black coal sometimes came to a grinding halt and touched the buffers of the truck in front, causing a series of dull

11

Joyce in Grimsby, 1940

metallic thuds, together with an elongated screech of brakes, which had a jarring effect on one's nerves.

It had been into one of these houses facing the railway siding that Bertie brought me. I followed him right to the top of the house and into a tiny flatlet, comprising one bedroom and a kitchen-cum-diner that looked out onto a depressing view of the railway line to the goods yard.

My wedding night was not the earth shattering saga that I had read about in books and seen on the films. It was in actual fact more like a comedy act. I laughed then, and I still smile now sometimes when I think of it. But Bertie did not think it was so funny.

After travelling all day and receiving a cold water reception at the end of it, I not only felt tired but peeved as well. The episode with the soldier had certainly not gone down well with Bertie and had set me off to a bad start. My mind was an uneasy jumble of thoughts as I realised that Bertie was not hurrying to get into bed, but was standing by the dressing-table and looking intently into the mirror.

I was yawning with fatigue from the day's journey, the clatter and click of the endless miles of rail track still hammering in my brain. All I wanted from the moment I'd met him was to feel the comfort of his arms around me, to be assured that I was loved and wanted, and to be taken care of. I felt neither sexually aroused nor passionate; all I wanted was a friendly cuddle.

I leaned over on to my elbow to see better. I was staggered to see him flexing his muscles and expanding his chest. Bertie was tall and extremely slim in those far off days. Any minute, I expected him to cough and fall over with all this heavy routine. It was when he began to fall face downwards onto the floor with such a belly flop that I thought the floorboards would split, and then, with laboured breathing, endeavour to execute press-ups, counting each one with clenched teeth, that I suppressed a little giggle. It was evident that he was out of puff and out of condition. I thought that if I encouraged him a little, he might get so exhausted that eventually he would stagger into bed and fall asleep. This was not what Bertie had in mind. What I was experiencing was a kind of ritual courtship dance. I had often read about the rather frenzied antics of the male scorpion displaying his sexual prowess to an uninterested female (or so I thought when she remained motionless). Bertie collapsed on the floor and I let out a shriek. It was so funny. If only he had seen the funny side of his antics, I know that the comedy might have helped us through. Gord had always stopped a serious situation from developing by making a joke. The joke, of course, was directed away from me. I suddenly felt uncomfortable and guilty. Bertie's ego had certainly been sandpapered that day, and I could see he was not amused. Our first day had been fraught, to say the least. Feeling far too tired to want any amorous overtures, I yawned and snuggled into the bedclothes. My head was still full of the clattering noise of the train and I was soon asleep and dreaming that I was on some kind of matrimonial collision course. I was in an express train that would not stop at the station which was my destination even though I was pulling the communication cord.

The next morning, the sounds of the coal trucks awakened me. That, along with the colourless grey of the day were my first impressions. Bertie was nowhere to be seen, but a note propped up by the side of the alarm clock informed me that he would be home for lunch at 12:30. I stretched in the comfortable bed and could easily have dozed off again, but hunger nudged me into activity and I got up to go in search of food and to explore my new surroundings. Except for tea in the caddy and a half jug of milk on the drainer, I found nothing substantial to eat, and finally concluded that my wifely duties would be commencing from that moment and I would have to get a move on if shopping needed to be done and a meal provided by the time specified on the note.

As I sipped my tea I looked around the room. It was well furnished and everything was new. There was a dining suite, two comfortable fireside chairs, and a sideboard to match. On the landing outside was a small stove, a sink with right hand drainer, and a cupboard above. A tiny boxroom revealed a toilet. No bathroom. This, I

14

discovered, was on the floor below. Since we occupied the two rooms on the top floor, our bedroom faced the railway siding in the front, and our lounge-cum-diner faced the gardens at the back.

I went downstairs to investigate who else lived in this quiet house. A pint-sized woman was brushing down the steps. She moved aside to let me pass. She nodded to me, smiling brightly and showing a large, loose tooth that protruded over her top lip when she did so. Wanting to be friendly as well as needing information, I sat down on one of the lower steps, enquired where the nearest shops might be, and was immediately educated as to where all the better and cheaper shops were situated. I was also directed to the market, a place that everybody frequented on Tuesday mornings.

She became very chatty and informative, telling me that she had been aware of our late arrival the night before. She had not wanted to bother us then, knowing that we must have been tired. Her name was Mrs Eden. She and her husband owned the house, and she had one daughter who was married but had gone and joined the Land Army and was now somewhere down south.

'Tis a nice flat, is that,' she said with a nod of her head towards the top of the house. 'Tis the daughter's,' she explained — then, leaning forward confidentially, she whispered, 'thought I'd do meself a mite good while the Army straightened our Gloria out.'

Here the loose tooth waggled up and down and Mrs Eden chuckled. Mr Eden was a trawler man and was away for long periods at a time. She walked with me to the door and pointed the way to the market.

I enjoyed the walk and found the market. I lingered longer than I had meant to. I was happy that morning, for I had bought a record and a pot of bright yellow chrysanths to brighten up the room. I had seen the radiogram in a corner and hoped it would work, hence the record. I completely lost track of the time and was horrified to find it was almost 12:30 and I still hadn't

15

shopped for items for lunch. Bertie would be there and waiting when I eventually got home. I purchased some apples from a barrow boy and then saw some yellow crumbly cheese on another stall. 'Cheese and some crusty bread,' I thought frantically, as I rushed from the still crowded market and back the way I had come. At the baker's, I recklessly bought six jam doughnuts, and dismally reflected that the twelve shillings I had started out with would now have to be juggled very carefully if it had to stretch right to the following Tuesday when my allowance was due. Perhaps Bertie would give me a little extra, I thought hopefully, as I let myself in and bounded up the steps, all three flights of them. Bertie was already in and waiting. He had made a cup of tea but did not offer me one. Instead, his face wore the pained expression of a hound who has been shut out all day.

I placed the flowers on the table hoping they might brighten him up as well as the room. I was careful at this stage not to strike a wrong note. I remembered last night and was eager to make amends.

'Crumps' Bertie exploded, 'You know I only have an hour.'

I quickly placed an apple on a plate and stole a glance. I really wanted to laugh because he was sitting there with a knife and fork in each hand, in eager anticipation. His eyes followed mine as I slowly brought the cheese into view and set it on a plate by the side of the apple.

So far there wasn't much evidence that he was going to enjoy anything as substantial as a cooked meal. Without looking at him, I began cutting 'navvy' slices of bread, in the hope that he would resign himself, as first days were always fraught. Perhaps the doughnuts just might clinch the deal. I even muttered something about cooking later and then he could hear my record. He choked on a piece of cheese and yelled,

'Record, woman! Do you mean to tell me that you have been spending my allowance on records?'

Before I could say another word, he had grabbed my

16

purse and made for the door muttering something about needing some money for a proper meal and not being sure what time he would be back.

I sat down nibbling at an apple, contemplating my next move. Without any money, there was nothing to be done. Besides, with no money for an evening meal, I was free for several long and boring hours. I walked to the radio-gram and placed my new record on the turntable. The strains of 'Tales from Vienna Woods' came loud and clear into the room. Nobody heard me cry as I ate my apple and cheese.

4 · *The Fish and Chip Saga*

Mr Eden was home. The house seemed to come alive as soon as he stepped through the front door. He was both good- natured and noisy. He went about banging doors and singing sea shanties at the top of his voice. When he loudly issued orders, everybody ran around as though they were pleased to be of service. He was skipper of his household as much as he was on his boat. He bellowed right up from the basement to me,

'Coom down to the kitchen, lass!'

When I arrived at the kitchen door, breathless after running down three flights of stairs, I was greeted by a middle-aged, bearded man in a striped butcher's apron brandishing a small, sharp-pointed knife. He was skil-fully and deftly slitting open a number of lemon sole and plaice and removing the backbones. The head and tail were also removed, and then with another quick flourish the fish was flopped back and forth in some creamy white batter. A large pan full of bubbly fat covered the whole of the stove. Into this went the fish, sizzling and turning a lovely golden brown. Periodically, he pulled down the handle of a small chip machine, feeding in whole potatoes.

The chips slithered out the other end into a bowl of cold water. When enough chips were done, he put them into a sieve and then straight into a massive chip pan on a special gas ring by the side of the stove.

Mrs Eden darted about laying the table for dinner. With dancing eyes and her front tooth wobbling, she exclaimed,

'Today is a right good day. Mr Eden is cooking fish and chips all round.' She told me,

'Go and fetch that young man of yours and bring him back down for dinner.' The smell of those fish and chips made me rush back to the flat to turn off the sausage and mash that I had prepared for Bertie's dinner. With a bit of luck, he could have that for tea. My mouth was already watering in anticipation of eating such delicious fresh fish. I opened my new book, there might be time to read a chapter before Bertie came in to dinner.

I was so absorbed in my book that I was unaware that Bertie had been standing in front of me for several seconds. He was so quiet, there had been no greeting, not even a peck on the cheek. He spoke at last. One word was all he said.

'Well?'

There was aggression in his tone. His aggression sparked off a need for me to retaliate.

'Well, what?' I said, equally belligerent.

The book was snatched out of my hands and thrown across the room.

'Where is my dinner?' The voice was quiet but held a veiled threat of reprisal if a satisfactory answer was not forthcoming.

'It's downstairs on the kitchen table, all ready for you to gobble up!' I said, as quietly as he had issued his question to me. I wanted to laugh at the puzzled look that came into his eyes, yet at the same time I wanted to pursue this cat-and-mouse game; to prolong the simple explanation that we had been invited down to dinner by Mr Eden. Bertie spluttered his usual overture about

18

wanting his meals on the dot and not expecting to have to guess where they were going to be located. I made the mistake of laughing when I began to explain that it was fish and chips for everybody today because Mr Eden was home. Instead of being pleased, he got angry, childishly accusing me of becoming lazy enough to expect other people to do my work. If that was the case, he said, I wouldn't need so much housekeeping money. My look of dazed incredulity was broken by the voice of Mrs Eden calling to us,

'Come on down now before your dinner gets cold and is spoiled.'

Bertie got stuck in and some of his surliness melted. He even managed a grunt of satisfaction by way of thanks as he laid down his knife and fork and left the room with a curt,

'See you tonight.'

Mr Eden eyed me after he had gone, especially when I began to thank him profusely for the excellent meal he had prepared for us all. To tell the truth, it was the first time in my entire life that I had seen any man cook a meal with dexterity and skill. On impulse, I blurted out,

'Would you show me how to fillet and skin a fish?'

'Eee lass,' he said, 'I'll do just that.'

I stood there blushing with embarrassment that I had to admit to this appalling lack of knowledge where the culinary art of skinning a fish was concerned. He leaned over and gently ruffled my hair.

'You'll learn to cook lass, long before your man learns his manners.'

'He finds it rather difficult to communicate,' I said breathlessly, rushing to Bertie's defence. 'You see, the ancient cavemen developed a well-defined set of grunts and groans which covered most things, including table manners and marital rights.'

Mr Eden's face wore a slightly puzzled frown until he saw that I was about to burst out laughing and he realised

19

I was joking. He thumped the table and gave a hearty chuckle and the pair of us burst out laughing.

'He's very young,' I smiled, 'and I'm working on him.'

The time spent at Stirling Street will always be remembered as a happy one, especially when in the company of Mr and Mrs Eden. We looked forward to the periods when he returned home from sea. There was always plenty of fresh fish and seafood, including lobster and crab. These he always put into a large pan of boiling water. I couldn't bear to watch and covered my ears so that I couldn't hear, for I swear I could hear them crying. Crab and lobster meat was the most delicious stuff I had ever tasted. I certainly ate like a king when Skipper Eden came bounding home.

It was a sad day when Gloria, their daughter, came home to find her flat had been invaded. One night we heard her angry voice shouting indignantly,

'If I had a bloody room I'd go sit in it.' Sadly, we knew it was time for us to move on.

5 · *On the Move Again*

On the following Monday I went into the town to collect my allowance from the sub-post office. A number of small streets led off the town's main road. The houses on these streets had no frontage, so the front doors came directly onto the pavement. They were tiny cottage-type buildings, comprising two rooms up and two down; squalid little houses built for the dock workers in the poorer quarter of town.

I collected my money from the counter, and exchanged a greeting with the counter hand. Turning round rather quickly, I collided with a young girl right behind me, almost knocking her over and, much to my consternation, spilling my money on the floor. She laughed and mentioned something about chucking my brass around, but gave up her place in the queue to bend down and help me to retrieve the coins that had rolled away. After that, I waited for her and we stood outside in the sunshine, talking easily and laughing about the incident. She told me her name was Margaret Burton. She had two boys, Tommy who was four and an older boy, Georgie, who was at school. Her husband was away in the army.

'Eee you're right bonny,' she said, 'coom and have a cup of tea.'

The range and the flagstones reminded me of South Road, but in that small kitchen she had made it bright and homely. I had at last found a friend and I was happy. When I looked around this bright little room, I felt the faint stirrings of a need to own something permanent like it for myself.

'Do you know of any rooms to let around this area?' I asked her suddenly.

'Tom Bradley's sister wants to let her house — her husband got killed at sea a while back. She's gone to live with her mother, but Tom Bradley has the key if you're interested.'

I couldn't believe my luck. I sat and stared.

'Nice warm little place is that,' she said, nodding towards the house two doors down. 'Finish your tea and I'll take you across to Tom Bradley. Ten shillings a week is what he's asking for it.'

Then she said, with a beam that lit up the whole of her face, 'We could be friends.'

Tom Bradley eyed me suspiciously. I was not a local and, what was worse, I was a Southerner. The further north one travelled, the more a 'foreigner' one became. Margaret, however, assured him that I was a friend of hers and that appeared to make things better. He led the way over the road and inserted the key into the lock of Number 7, Clyde Street.

The tiny front room smelt damp and musty. A faded carpet covered a stone floor. There was a radiogram in

21

one corner and a three piece suite of doubtful origin taking up the rest of the space. The kitchen was the same in design as Margaret's, and reminded me of home. I wanted to sit in front of the range with a fire half way up the chimney. I wanted to hear the kettle singing on the hob.

I glanced towards the scullery, which was a glass covered lean-to. I noted a black stove and cold tap with a sink and drainer. A dolly tub complete with a wooden basher stood in the corner. The drains didn't smell so good. A great air raid shelter took up the whole square of garden. Margaret said it was for the whole rank of seven houses. Tom Bradley was the Air Raid Warden.

'I'll look after you, ducks,' he said confidently.

I said I would take the house and turned to hug Margaret, who seemed as pleased as I was that our friendship should be cemented in this way.

Once more, the small brown tin trunk was transferred, this time from Stirling Street to Clyde Street and we moved into that tiny house — a whole house, however tiny, was better than rooms. It was here that I began to think of myself as a real housewife. Bertie, too, was more relaxed and settled, and he would sit by a great roaring fire that he himself became adept at lighting. Members of the crew would sometimes pop round for a chat, and I would proudly show them into the parlour and feel very married and, at that time, happy.

Margaret remained a loyal friend. Most days we'd have coffee and biscuits together. One day we had a heavy storm. The drains blocked and water came right up into the lean-to kitchen. The smell was awful. Margaret assured me that it had been happening for as long as she could remember. Laughing at my look of disgust, she helped me to sweep out the evil smelling seepage.

She didn't laugh in the weeks that followed, when her youngest lad went down with diptheria. Tommy was flushed with a high temperature when we wheeled him to the doctor, who immediately admitted him to the fever

22

hospital. We went every week to see Tommy, but were only allowed to wave to him from the window. His tearful little face looking down at us made us both cry. Margaret said,

'We make a right pair of loonies, don't we?'

I am sure she appreciated my tears, though. We made a cake on the day he came home. It was my first attempt at icing, and I proudly placed it on the table for him, with Tommy written in pink. He promptly told me it should have been in blue, but he said the cake was good and kissed me.

The sirens wailed that night, but it was like a party, with everybody singing and the women taking it in turns to make jugs of hot cocoa. Tom Bradley would give us a minute to minute account of the damage that the aircraft were causing in the town. Such and such a building was blazing away, or part of the dock was their objective, he would say.

We became familiar with the low throb of enemy aircraft. Tom Bradley had a real sense of humour and kept us all happy by telling jokes every time the dull thud of a bomb falling could be heard. We sang songs and even played cards down in that shelter in Clyde Street. Afterwards, the whole street would meet to talk about the night's activity. We all helped each other and commiserated when a relative or son became a casualty, or a telegram arrived with the news of the death of a loved one.

On the nights that Bertie went off to the pub with the boys, I stayed with Margaret. During the day, we took Tommy to the park. In the evenings I stayed with her, knitting or sewing, or just talking. So far I had never been to the pub with Bertie and his crew mates. Margaret commented on this one night and suggested that I should insist that I go with him. Bored and irritable with the long hours on my own, I pleaded with him to take me to the pictures. He thought for a while and then said he would perhaps be able to manage it a week from then.

23

He also intimated that he considered he had bestowed on me a favour by bringing me to this great East Coast town. All I had to do all day was to explore the place and get to know people and make friends. He wished that was all he had to do. I told him I was not impressed with this bloody cold East town, and unless he could spare me a bit more of his precious time I was packing up and going home. He thought about that then came up with,

'You can't. You haven't any money.'

I instantly regretted the next remark, when I stupidly confessed that I had been saving two shillings a week to go home for a visit.

'Man and wife should have no secrets from each other, where have you hidden it?'

'No secret,' I said innocently, 'It's in one of the china bowls on the dressing table.'

'Get your coat on,' he said at last, putting the money in his pocket. 'But don't think I am going to make a habit of taking you to the pub every time I go out with the boys.'

I had won that round, but not for long.

The lads were already in the pub when we arrived, seated round a table that was swilling with beer. The brown liquid ran in tiny rivulets down on to the floor. Room was made for us with a great scraping of chairs and another round of drinks was called. A look in my direction and a hurried consultation finally brought a dainty, tiny, narrow-necked glass filled with a thick yellow substance which Bertie whispered to me was called egg flip and had to be sipped slowly, and not tossed back in one gulp.

The crew of High Speed Launch 111 were a motley crowd. Bertie was a Deck Hand together with Billy Davis, a Cockney who interspersed every sentence with 'Cor blimey, stone the crows.' Wally Walsh was a Leading Hand which was one step up on the promotional ladder. He didn't speak much, and gave the impression of being surly and sullen. In complete contrast there was the

coxswain, who just about laughed at everything including his own jokes, and was appropriately nicknamed
'Smiler Smithy'. These four stuck together like glue and
formed a boozing quartet, each bolstering the other's ego
by continually asserting that as they were fighting and
bleeding for their country, they were entitled to drink
and be merry today, because tomorrow they might all be
dead. They called Bertie 'Jack' or sometimes 'Fred'. I
think he responded to almost anything after he had
supped a few ales.

The room was smoke filled and noisy, and a blond lad
was playing the piano. Small knots of airmen were singing bawdy songs in slurred, half tipsy voices. A dish cloth
came whizzing through the air. Catching it expertly with
one hand, Billy Davis muttered one of his famous 'Cor
blimey, stone the crows' expressions, then began mopping up the beer that lay in pools all over the table.
Amidst loud laughter, he wrung out the cloth into an
empty beer mug, then threw it back towards the bar,
where it missed the barman and landed on the glass
behind him with a muffled thud.

I sipped my drink and found it pleasant. Every time a
round of drinks was called, another tot of egg flip was
added for me. I now had six of the things lined up like
soldiers in front of me. By the time I had consumed the
third tot of this delicious yellow stuff, I was amazed to
find that the whole room had taken on a brighter dimen-
sion. As I looked round at Bertie's friends, I was fasci-
nated by their company and every word they spoke
seemed to hold a deeper meaning. I found myself leaning forward so that I could catch every one. The whole
room became enhanced with colours which heightened
the swaying figures like something from a real life drama,
all with a special meaning for me.

When Billy Davis called my beloved 'Fred', I had a
sudden and impulsive urge to set the record straight. I
leaned across the beer-soaked table and said in a very
loud voice,

25

'His mother calls him Darling Bertie.'

A great roar of laughter went up from the crew around the table but Bertie looked uncomfortable. His face reddened and his quick glance in my direction let me know he was both embarrassed and angry. In my happy state, I thought it was about time that I gave him a proper name, a real man's name. 'Well, you can all call him what you like but he has a very nice second Christian name, John, and that is what I shall call him from now on.'

The crew looked on, still grinning, but I think they approved. From that moment on, he was John to me, Fred or Jack to his mates, Darling Bertie to his mother, and just plain Bert to his sister and two brothers.

Out of the corner of my eye, I saw Flying Officer Bowen and Sergeant Brodie making their way to our table. By the state they were already in, it could safely be assumed that they had frequented all the pubs within a five mile radius. They were of the same stature and build, both about the same age, in their early thirties, and where one went, the other followed. Bowen was definitely the public school character.

'What ho, chaps, we're all in this together, what?'

He had a smooth, round face on which he had culti-vated a rather fine moustache, which reminded me of a colonial officer from the Boer War. He was a charmer, he oozed it like cream from a doughnut. Brodie, on the other hand, looked surly and sulky and his face lacked charm of any kind. He was as battered as a bruiser boxer. With his cap pulled well down, and a cane under his arm, he would have been more at home on the parade ground drilling raw recruits and bawling,

'You might break yer mother's 'art, but you won't break MINE!'

They were as different in character as chalk and cheese, yet surprisingly enough, these two were inseparable.

John got to his feet to introduce me and also to offer Brodie a chair, because it was evident that he was swaying so unsteadily that it was the safest place for him at the moment.

'This is my wife, Sir,' John began, and Flying Officer Bowen waved his hand airily around trying hard to focus on me, whilst holding on to the table.

'Welcome aboard, little lady, welcome aboard.' Then he addressed his crew, his face now wreathed in smiles, 'This calls for little drinkies, what?'

John went with him to the bar and he called for yet another round of beers and, of course, one more soldier tot of egg flip for me.

Meanwhile Brodie was sitting there looking slightly glassy-eyed and foolishly trying to reach out to grasp a pint mug of beer that was directly in front of him and not quite making it because of his blurred vision. I sat watching him intently and giggling at his foolish antics. Presently, he leaned back in his chair and without warning slid effortlessly down on to the floor and under the table.

Bowen returned a little while later and looked stupidly around for his drinking partner. The look of bemused anxiety on his face when he beheld only the empty chair made me almost choke with mirth. I stole a look at Brodie's inert form under the table and vowed I would not tell a soul where he was. This would be my great secret. Each time I looked at Flying Officer Bowen and saw the puzzlement on his face, I almost exploded with laughter. Bowen was so drunk, I thought, he doesn't even know where he left Brodie. At this point, it became very urgent for me to go to the loo. As I made my way to the door, I was surprised to find that I was not walking in a very straight line. However, as the room was crowded, I made the door without mishap, and then tried to manoeuvre the four steps up to the Ladies. The step instead came up to meet me. This, I thought, was a novel experience, going up and down several times before a sudden urge to be sick prompted a dash to the loo, where, with my two arms embracing the pedestal, I was horribly and revoltingly sick.

I became conscious of the fact that I was sitting on a dirty floor strewn with pieces of San Izal toilet paper that had been pulled from the china holder on the wall. With shafts of pain going through my head, I pulled myself up from the floor and made my way to the tiny sink outside in the corridor. I washed my face in cold water. I couldn't find a towel, so mopped most of the surplus water off with a tiny square of handkerchief that I found up my sleeve. A door at the end of the hall, when opened, revealed a small enclosure at the rear of the pub and I leaned against the wall to take in a few deep breaths of cold night air. It seemed that, as I stood there, other shadowy figures stood facing and talking quietly to the wall. I giggled when I realised that these silent bods were, in fact, relieving themselves. It was here that John found me. I could tell instantly that he was displeased with me by the way he tutted and said 'Oh crumps!' when I was sick again. All those motionless shapes seemed to melt into the shadows and John couldn't get me through the pub gates fast enough and out into the road.

'Can't take you anywhere,' he grumbled.

I couldn't answer him because my head felt like bursting and what was worse, the sky wasn't where it should have been.

'Never again!' I vowed, as John tried to extricate me from a lamp-post. I sat down in the gutter feeling so ill I wanted to die.

'You can only reach a point,' I wailed miserably into the night, 'then you have to come back again.'

John eyed me grimly. I knew I would never be asked to go to the pub again.

I also knew where Brodie was.

6 · *Black Outs and Air Raids*

After the episode at the pub, I was convinced that I was not a drinking woman. John, on the other hand, did come from a drinking family. I argued with myself that, with him being the only married man in that boozy quartet, he should be spending more time at home with me. Reviewing the events of that night, John said,

'I hardly like to convey to you the comments of the crew, Pet,' then proceeded to tell me just the same. With sickening clarity I learned just what they thought of me. It was their considered opinion that I was a very nice girl, but Billy Davis thought I would be more at home in the Salvation Army Band playing a tambourine. The other three embellished the picture by adding a bonnet and mockingly singing 'bringing in the sheaves'. I immediately burst into tears and told him how horrid I thought he was. He stopped laughing and replied that he was only joking. Then he pulled from his pocket a grubby handkerchief together with a couple of fag ends, and said,

'Dry your eyes, my Pet, and tonight I'll take you to the flicks.' He gave me a peck on the cheek and disappeared round the corner, only to reappear seconds later to call out cheerfully,

'Be ready at 6:30 sharp.' I couldn't wait for the evening to come; the afternoon dragged on and on. At 6:30 on the dot I was ready and waiting, sitting in the wooden arm chair with my hat and coat on. My gloves and a torch lay on the table. To venture out in the blackout without the welcome beam from the torch would present a hazard.

John was ten minutes late, despite the fact that it was he who had insisted upon my punctuality. As we hurried along the darkened streets, I grumbled a little. It was very cold and the wind blew in sudden little icy gusts that made my face smart and my eyes water. I shivered and

The crew of High Speed Launch 111 in Grimsby Docks, early 1940. John is at far left; Bowen and Brodie centre front

pulled up the collar of my coat to help shield my face. John pulled me closer to him and then covered the whole of my face with his big warm hands. I was now quite unable to see where I was walking. He was guiding me, instructing me when to negotiate the kerb stones to cross the streets and roads. In a devil may care mood, he played a joke on me, telling me quietly and earnestly that we were coming to a flight of steps.

'Up, up,' he directed, so that I immediately complied by lifting my knee quite high from the ground. When I discovered that I was not making contact with any kind of step and my high stepping antics sent him into hysterics, I gave him a well-deserved thump. The pair of us after that rocked about with laughter so much that we had to stop in a doorway to recover our breath. Then we both ran along the road to the cinema because John whispered,

'It's a Bette Davis film and she's got such a sexy voice.'

The cinema was a bible black blob. No bright neon

emblazoned the names of the stars and the feature film revolving round and round in a star-studded endless silver square. These had been extinguished at the onset of the war. There wasn't even the all important grey liveried attendant with the gold braid epaulets on his shoulder shouting on the steps the number of seats available in the balcony. A very full, pleated blackout curtain now draped the great doors at the entrance to the foyer. Once inside their voluptuous folds, you came face to face with a high plywood partition forming a corridor along which the patrons shuffled. A sharp turn to the right at the end of this makeshift entrance led to the dimly lit paybox. So low was the light in that gloom, that it was advisable to have the right amount of money for the ticket; sometimes the keenest eye found it difficult to discern whether the right change had been given.

Once inside, nothing seemed to have changed. The Pathe Gazette News had already started, and we found seats right at the back, where we divested ourselves of our coats and snuggled up to one another. I was surprised and delighted when John placed a bag of sweets in my lap. Sweets were on ration and we usually gobbled up the two meagre ounces that we were allowed each week. John always seemed to be able to conjure up extra coupons from thin air, and I would often tease him with this. In fact, his boyish charm made him a favourite with the older women who worked in the NAAFI and they often gave him their sweet ration.

Sometimes, I saw through the blatant propaganda of the newsreel and would irritate John when I muttered, 'Just as if!' I was about to open my mouth to utter scathingly, 'More lies!', when he stopped me with a very short, sharp,

'Sshhh!'

I deliberately rustled the bag to extract a sweet and annoy him still further by sucking away furiously, but I was relaxed and happy. Snuggled up by the side of him, I was soon immersed in the great escapism of the film.

We blinked when the lights suddenly went up in the middle of the feature film and a message was flashed on the screen announcing that an air-raid warning had just sounded. All those wishing to take advantage of the shelters across the road could now do so as quickly as possible, through the exits provided. The film would continue for those people wishing to stay behind. They were reminded that they did so at their own risk.

I pulled back the red plush seat and began putting on my coat. I knew that in the event of an air-raid, John would have to make his way to the docks as quickly as possible. I watched the hunched figures slowly filing out through the exits. The beam of light directed onto the screen from the powerful projector now caught and held great waves of cigarette smoke and dust. When they had turned on the cinema lights, it seemed not just to have severed the film sequence, but shattered a fantasy, an intrusion that made me feel irritable and angry. Through the endless yards of celluloid, reality had intruded — reminding us that outside, a war was still going on, and we must not forget it. Not even in the cinema could we dream, perchance to sleep.

Once outside again, we shivered in the cold night air. The beams from dozens of searchlights criss-crossed, searching the skies. In the distance, we heard the low throb of enemy aircraft. Holding hands, we ran as fast as our legs could carry us through the darkened street until we came to Clyde Street. John grabbed his bike from the shed, and I had time only to call,

'Take care!'

Tom Bradley almost pushed me into the shelter as the first stick of bombs fell very, very close with a sickening THUMP! THUMP! THUMP!

7 · *Chicken Soup*

Just so long as I didn't ask to go to the pub with John and the lads, it was taken for granted that I could be taken to the flicks instead. These special little treats came every six weeks, or every time my tawny-sherry coloured eyes flashed a warning signal to my spouse that he was neglecting me.

'Alright, my plum,' he announced one breakfast time, with his mouth full of shredded wheat, 'Be ready at 6:30 sharp.'

It was Margaret who had told me that it was a Bogart film. She asked me to take particular notice of how many fags he lit up, took one puff from, and then threw away.

'Must cost him a small fortune,' she mocked.

I sat nervously tapping my fingers on the arm of the chair when John had not arrived at a quarter to seven. At 8:00, I simmered with controlled fury. By the time the clock broke an uneasy silence and chimed the hour of 9:00, I was hopping mad and ready to do battle. I poked viciously at the fire that I had so carefully banked so that it would be warm and cosy to return to. I had filled a blue, two pound sugar bag with small coal and potato peelings (a domestic tip I learned from Margaret, for I was a proper wife now). The fire at once sprang into life and sent showers of sparks and flame up through the wide aperture of the chimney. Nothing for it now but to take off my outdoor clobber, have a drink and go to bed. Contrariness followed the anger. No, I would not go to bed, I would stay up and have it out with John. I would show him that he could not treat me in this way. The unfairness of being taken out once every six weeks when he could walk out almost every night appeared to make the scales of justice topple alarmingly to one side. I sat there fuming, with the fire getting lower and lower and the room colder and colder.

Just as I decided for the second time to go to bed, I heard the key in the lock of the front door and somebody heaving their weight against it to make it open. I guessed it was raining outside because the dampness caused the door to stick and nothing but a hefty shove would make it open. I was not surprised to see four very wet and sloshed airmen almost fall into the tiny parlour and stagger towards the kitchen, looking bleary-eyed and stupid. Out of the third and fourth buttons of John's greatcoat hung something that dangled, long and flabby, that he was grasping with both hands. When he saw my startled look, he came towards me undoing all the buttons and disclosing the rather flaccid carcass of a very dead chicken.

'For you, my pet,' he slurred, then sat down heavily on the sofa, where he kept repeating childishly, 'I've been a bad, bad boy.'

The others by this time had arranged themselves along the wall, swaying and flaying around. When Billy Davis suddenly cried out,

'Cor, stine the crows!' and made for the outside loo, they all turned and followed him, looking like an out-sized game of follow the leader. When he tripped over the steps, I heard,

'A tishoo, a tishoowe all fall down.' I looked at the dead chicken in my lap and suddenly wanted to laugh at the foolish antics of these four grown men. Churchill's famous speech about so much being owed by so many to so few could not have been inspired by a spectacle such as this. I let the chicken fall to the floor, already I was doubled up with mirth. When the lads eventually returned, they came back each with a hand on the shoulder of the one in front. Billy Davis was leading and his hand was stuck out in front. They were incapable of recounting the incident of the bird, which I retrieved from the floor and took into the kitchen to soak in a bowl of cold water. John by this time had keeled over and was snoring away. I left him there and proceeded to climb the stairs to go to bed.

I told the others that they could doss up in the parlour if they wished or try to make it to their digs if they thought they could. I had a last impression of three white faces at the bottom of the stairs, hands clasped about each other's necks, trying to stand upright, all three slurring at my retreating back,

'Thank sho much, Mrs Shtorey. Much appreshiated, Mrs Shtorey. Goo nigh, Mrs Shtorey.'

The following morning, four sobered up airmen gave a credible account of the previous night. Over their bowls of shredded wheat and plates of toast, it transpired that it was Billy Davis who coerced John into going into a Working Mans Club to play a quick game of tombola. One of the tombola prizes was a chicken, and several of the men who won it had already handed it back to be raffled again in order to swell the kitty. John by this time was tipsy and feeling maudlin and sentimental about spoiling my evening, and thought it would be a good idea to win the bird as a peace offering. Everybody in the club now knew all about the sad little woman left crying all alone in Clyde Street. Cheered on by his crew mates and the rest of the men at the club, they stayed there till turning out time, endeavouring to win the wretched thing. Eventually, I think it was given to him. They never did tell me what it cost them for that evening's work, but I did have the pleasure of his company for a whole week, when it was obvious he was skint and couldn't afford to wander out. I made soup with the bird, which was all it was fit for. I served it up every night until it was nearly gone, and demanded that my nights out at the pictures should be increased to once a month. To my surprise, he agreed. He even said he would take me that very night. He looked down at the table cloth and said apologetically,

'But I won't have any more of that soup for tea tonight. It repeats on me.'

35

8 · *Problems and Pregnancy*

I knew I was pregnant that first morning I was sick. The previous week I'd had my suspicions because when I had walked through the market with all the stalls piled high with fruit, the smell had brought on a slight feeling of nausea. Feeling wretched, I confided in Margaret. She only laughed and told me that the shop at the top of the road sold the best selection of baby wool, and that one cure for baby blues was to get the old needles clicking. I yelled at her that I was not happy about the patter of baby feet in pale blue bootees, especially right bang in the middle of a war. I personally thought it was the dumbest thing that could have befallen me.

That night, I confronted John and told him what I thought and how I felt. On both counts no sympathy was forthcoming. He spouted some dirge about women having babies all the time and not making half the fuss that I was, and if nobody had a baby because there was a war on, the world would be in a sorry state. I replied coldly that it was my considered opinion that women had no control over their own bodies and that if he had taken the opportunity to use the 'thingies' that the Service dished out so cheaply and so easily, with a little more consideration for me, we would not be facing each other at this moment like a pair of fighting cocks, and the question of how and when a child could be born without a home need not be discussed.

John went off to the pub to try to find the answer to that one over a pint. His pals commiserated, and reassured him,

'Women are unreasonable at times like that.'

They brought him home very late that night, extremely drunk, and put him in a chair.

'Leave him, Missus,' they said. 'Let him sleep it off.'

36

He could have stayed there forever for all I cared. I wasn't happy either.

Margaret came with me to the clinic. It was October again. I had been in Grimsby a whole year. As we set off to catch a bus to the town, the air was crisp and cold. The leaves on the trees were already falling, flying in rapid succession one after another. The wind blew them along in front of us and piled them high against the shelter of the wall. They came flying through the air looking like migrating birds. I have always loved this monththe colours of the leavesearthy browns through to shades of gold; harvest time and the month of the long shadows. This was the month that my parents had married. I remembered my mother had told me about the huge pots of yellow and bronze chrysanthemums in the chapel windows and how the sun had shone on the altar rail. I felt homesick and wanted to cry.

The clinic confirmed I was twelve weeks pregnant.

Towards the end of October we had a howling gale with gusts of wind up to fifty miles an hour. Tiles and chimney pots were blown around and came crashing down. The wind shrieked as though all the fiends in hell were abroad that night. Miraculously, the only damage sustained by our little glass lean-to was five missing panes of glass, leaving a hole about four feet wide in the centre.

Tom Bradley assured us that he could obtain the glass quite cheaply and that it would only be a matter of a few shillings if John could fix the glass back in. He was so convinced that he had settled the deal amicably and with the minimum amount of fuss, that he was amazed when his good intentions met with stubborn resistance from John, who said he had no intentions of fixing the glass, or paying for it. An act of God, in his opinion, should be covered by insurance. Any replacement cost should be met by the person who owned the house and it was their sole responsibility.

Tom Bradley was furious. He thought John's attitude was boorish and arrogant. Damage as negligible as this was too trivial to be an insurance claim, and what he had suggested was a compromise between two civilised men. John did not budge from his position, neither did he even glance up from the paper he was reading. Tom Bradley was so angry that he stuttered that we could vacate his premises as soon as he had time to write out a formal notice to quit. I said nothing, but knew Tom would be as good as his word.

In due course, we received the notice to quit the premises. My tearful attempts at trying to make John see reason failed, and when I finally yelled at him that I would have no place to bring a baby home to, he infuriated me still further by quietly stating that he was not going to be intimidated by Tom Bradley or emotionally blackmailed by me. If we had to move, he was sure of finding other accommodation as good as this, if not better. The drains would not be good for a baby, anyway.

Margaret commiserated once more with me and said that she had told Tom Bradley about my condition and urged him to reconsider his rash step in telling us to go. He had shown concern at her news about the baby and assured Margaret that he had no wish to be thought of as a tyrant, especially as he liked me and knew how much I liked the little house. If John would meet him halfway, he would forget all about it.

Alas! There were no half-measures where John was concerned and as long as I lived with him I would always have to cope with this stubborn streak. In a man who was otherwise so often gentle and easy-going, his sudden obstinacy often came as a surprise. He would dig in his heels and refuse to budge and it infuriated me, and made the sparks fly.

So whilst Margaret and I clung to each other and cried at the severed friendship about to take place, John took his bike to go in search of fresh lodgings.

At this point in my pregnancy, I developed a compulsion for cockles. I would purchase a pint of them at a time from a wet fish shop, and on the way home tear a hole in the bag to get these fat little morsels in my fingers to stuff them into my mouth. Margaret and I made jokes about the baby who might have a cockle-shaped birth-mark because of my desire for the taste of them.

That last week at Clyde Street was made as pleasant as possible. I spent hours going round to the six other occupants saying goodbye to them. Bessy, who lived at the end of the terrace, made delicious ice cream with eggs and custard powder, frozen with ice cubes packed at the bottom of a metal container. We consumed this by the spoonful, and Margaret's two boys would come in for a share with shiny eyes and giggles.

Sadly I said goodbye to the first little home that I had known. I hugged Margaret and told her I would return to see her from time to time. I pulled the tin trunk from the cupboard under the stairs. It was heavier now, for a few more things had been added to it.

It was ready and waiting for yet one more move.

9 · *Mill Lane*

Clyde Street had been a humble place and the people in that small terrace of seven houses were God-fearing folk, generous and ready to share the little that they had, all eager and ready to help a stranger. Danger and the war brought us all close together in a companionship and bond not easy to sever or to forget.

In comparison, Mill Lane was situated in the poorest part of the Dock area, and my first impression of my new surroundings was that they left a lot to be desired. A fat, squat, round gasometer, painted a dirty dark green, stood out stark and ugly against the skyline at the far end of the lane. The lane ended in a mud track and led into the premises in which this unlovely giant was situated. On this particular day, with the wind in the wrong direction, the smell emanating from this silent monster was awful.

Six houses only remained in this road, and these faced a boarded up bomb site on the other side, behind which was the rubble and remains of the facing terrace that had once housed people who had lived and laughed and loved. Now only a wooden boarding hid the silent bricks scattered casually around. No life there now; the devastation could be hidden but not the depression that seemed to hover and brood over the whole lane.

With a sinking heart, I let my gaze follow the boarding to where a single gas lamp leaned crazily at the end of a pavement. I smiled, for it was apparent that the bomb blast had not quite succeeded in dislodging it completely from its cemented moorings. Ironically, neither had it touched the pub on the other side of the pavement. This stood intact and untouched with its wooden sign swinging in the slight autumn breeze — THE RISING SUN. Maybe someone had a sense of humour and had concluded that if the gasometer obscured the view of this shining orb in motion, he could go into the pub and be consoled with a pint. The boarding began again right next to the pub. Half mockingly, I said to myself,

'Ha, ha — missed!'

I had heard that a bomb could never fall on the same spot twice. As I looked around that devastated place I felt I wouldn't like to push my luck. As we neared the remaining houses, the smell of cabbage wafted upon the air. This, coupled with the smell from the gasometer, made me wrinkle up my nose in disgust. A dog nosing about in an open bin that had been placed outside one of the houses suddenly succeeded in tipping the bin over and scattering the contents all over the pavement. A voice from the interior shouted at the dog and a missile that looked like an old boot came flying out of the open doorway.

'Git outofit!'

The dog yelped and sidled round the corner just out

of sight, not intending to move too far away, but determined to play scavenger for any titbits hidden in the bin.

Before I followed John into the very last house, I gave a disgusted last look around and said sarcastically,

'Well, at least the pub is near enough away for me to know where to find you, and the bomb site is the ideal spot for your child to play on. The gasometer, too, is far better than the drains at Clyde Street. I must congratulate you on finding me the ideal spot.'

He did not reply and I followed him, firm-faced, angry and resentful.

Mrs Robinson owned the house. She came down the stairs to greet us. She was tall and very thin. She had grey hair and slate grey eyes. The pallor of her skin was grey and she panted and wheezed alarmingly, for she suffered dreadfully with asthma. She had to sit on a chair and recover from the effort of descending the stairs before she could speak to us. When she smiled, her whole face lit up. It was like an April sun sweeping over a field and transforming the day into a mellow gold. I nicknamed her 'The Grey Lady', but I loved always seeing the smile light up those slate grey eyes.

There was one other occupant in the house. This was an old lady who lived in the front room. Mrs Robinson indicated by putting her forefinger to her head that she was 'slightly cuckoo', but harmless. I concluded that she really meant that the old lady was confused. Between gasps and pants for breath, she showed us our room and apologised for its smallness. She indicated with a nod of her head the front of the house where the old lady lived.

'She can't last out much longer, then perhaps you would like both rooms.'

Our room faced the yard. A path extending down about fifty yards to the back gate and a wall dividing the houses was the only view from the french doors, which could be opened out into the yard. A bed settee took up the side of one wall. We did have a grate with an oven in one side. In the recess by the window there was a sideboard on the top of which had been placed a piece of flowered oilcloth and now housed cups and saucers, and a tray with a tea pot and jug. Underneath was an assortment of pots and dishes. She breathlessly assured me that I must ask for anything that she had omitted to provide. She showed me the tiny scullery that she said they all had to share.

'Not that I shall ever be in your way,' she smiled, 'I have my own bits and pieces upstairs and don't come down unless I have to.' She looked across the room. 'I guess if your name is on one of those whizz bangs you've had it,' she said stoically, then pointed to the deep cupboard under the stairs where she had placed a mattress. 'I have no need for a shelter, I'd die trying to get into one. You will be as safe as anywhere under here.'

I wanted to ask her why she stayed in a place that was so dangerous and obviously bad for her asthmatical condition, but she was already tiring and heading for the stairs. She called over her shoulder for us to make ourselves at home and to make a cup of tea. When I called after her would she like one as well, she could only nod. She was sitting on the top step, trying to get her breath, but shook her head vigorously when I asked if there was anything I could do to help.

When the bed settee was pulled down that night, it took up the whole room and even extended into the grate. The mattress was lumpy and hurt my back. When I wanted the toilet in the middle of the night, I had to crawl over John, negotiate the dark scullery and unbolt the back door into the yard. The sky was full of stars — there was no raid that night. I thought of Margaret and knew I would miss the jollity of the crowd of 12 or so people from the terrace — Tom Bradley and his warm-hearted humour that gave us the confidence to laugh in the face of danger; the jugs of steaming hot cocoa and the cards that we played. Sometimes even this was forgotten when the whine of a stack of bombs falling much too close for comfort made us hold our breath.

I saw less and less of John. In my hostile mood, he kept a discreet distance. He now had his meals at the NAAFI, where he commented that he could be sure of coming into contact with a smiling face and not a scowling one. Without a soul to talk to except Mrs Robinson and the old lady in the front room, I was not only lonely, I was unhappy. I resolved to go and see Margaret. She was overjoyed to see me and said we should take the boys into Cleethorpes on the bus. I had never been to the beach before, which was about six miles away on the far side of the town.

It was November. The sun was warm when we set off, although it held a tang of winter in its pale rays. In sheltered places it was quite pleasant for walking, and the boys kept up a lively and excited chatter about the sand dunes they were going to show me and the fun they had in the summer when the pier and amusements were open. When we finally arrived at the long stretch of sand, they raced on ahead to find flat-topped pebbles that would skim along the surface of the water when expertly thrown in a certain way.

A cold wind now blew off the grey murky waters of that East coast, whipping up the tide's wavelets so that they splashed angrily and noisily up on to the beach, staining the mud-coloured sand an even darker wet and shiny hue. I had a sudden mental picture of the softer contours of our south coast, with its tiny inlets and bays, rock pools and walks along the cliff paths. I felt very homesick. The boys let out a wild whoop and pointed to the sand dunes a little to the left of us. Margaret said we would race the boys to the dunes.

'It will give you an appetite for your dinner.'

She laughed at the expression on my face, but I set off after the boys, who bounded away like agile young monkeys. When we got to the dunes, the boys began digging and scooping out a large hole whilst we hid behind a great wall of sand to shelter us from the keen wind that would suddenly blow the sand particles and sting our faces. I watched the boys for a while, playing their fantasy games in the big hole that they had now converted into an imaginary speed car. Sometimes they sparred with each other on the sandy slope of the dunes and rolled over and over like two young wayward puppies.

'Do you want a boy?' Margaret interrupted my thoughts to ask.

'No,' I replied without hesitation, 'I want a girl to make up for the sister I never had. A sister just like you,' I went on impulsively, and we both giggled and hugged each other.

I turned towards the sea and watched the turbulent and angry swell of the autumnal tide. The wind was stronger now and it was obvious that we would soon have to make tracks for home. I shouted into the wind as loud as I could:

'I am going to have a girl just like me who I can show all the things that I love, and she will love them too and I will never be lonely again.'

The wind was blowing Margaret's hair up and around her face. She attempted to hold back the wayward strands and, still laughing, shouted that she hoped I would get my wish.

'I know I will!' was my reply, 'I know I will.'

We chased the two boys back over the sandy beach. We passed the piles of coloured canvas deck chairs piled and stacked and soon to be covered for the winter. The beach was almost deserted now and a cold wind blew. We were glad when the bus stage was reached and as we stood there waiting for it to come along, I thought of the coming spring that would bring all things new again and with it would bring Motherhood for me.

10 · *The Flame of Reality*

Autumn slipped into winter, with high winds that whipped up the green tipped waves of the North Sea so that
they pounded the harbour wall and sent spray high in
the air and over into the roadway, making the way im-
passable. Cars and pedestrians were diverted via another
route. During the summer months, this had been a
favourite walk of mine. I loved the salt breeze, the cry
of the gulls, all the activity that a busy harbour brings.
Most of all, I loved the vast expanse of sea and sky, one
great space where my imagination could soar and go on
forever.

There had been that day when two planes had appeared
from behind a feathery, frothy white cloud. The sun was
glinting on the wing tips, making both planes look as
though they had been shot with silver. We stood there by
the harbour walls with our eyes shaded against the sun
to watch this drama being enacted over the water: the
attacker and the attacked. As one streaked away, veering
sideways to avoid the staccato burst of gun fire that could
be plainly heard by those standing below on the ground,
the other again zoomed upwards. There was a moment
when both planes blotted out the sun so that they seemed
like a purple shadow against the sky. In that momentary
silence there was a tiny cough and a splutter as if the
engine of that plane was emitting a half-strangled death
cry before finally bursting into flames and beginning its
dizzy spiral descent into the cold waters below.

Witnessing this tragic episode affected me deeply. I
watched the bystanders who were beginning to disperse,
some shaking their heads sadly before walking on to
attend to their own affairs. I felt suddenly very cold and
empty. I wanted an answer to all this insane killing and
aggression. I was very aware of being pregnant and
creating life, while men were wasting it. Women were the

creators and the carers; men destroyed. I found myself praying desperately that my baby would be a girl, then hopelessly wondering if one day in the future, she too might be praying for an answer to how she fitted into this ceaseless futile round of warfare and aggression and senseless human sacrifice.

John had joined a branch of the Services that saved lives instead of taking them, and I admired him for that. Whether it was 'one of ours' or the enemy made no difference to the crews of the Air Sea Rescue Service. And when Jerry had been fished out of the freezing waters of the North Sea and wrapped in blankets and been given a warming cuppa, even the language barrier could be broken by handshakes and smiles and the exchange of photographs of dear ones.

I thought, all men must stop to eat, and all of them some time or another must forget the combat to lie down to sleep and recharge their own bodies. Like small children they came home to us to be fed and loved. And what was I? I looked out over the grey expanse of water and felt small and insignificant.

During the winter months, it would be the turn of the heavier deep sea launches of the Royal Navy to respond to any distress calls. The High Speed Launches of the Royal Air Force were not sea-going craft and could only operate in the Humber and inshore waters. The turbulence of the North Sea could smash these frail craft to pulp. It was on a bitter January night, when a keen cold wind blew from the North that whipped up the waves and made them choppy, that the lads were all down in the fo'c's'le playing poker. There was a fiver in the kitty and from the grave faces of the men and the nervous twitch of nicotine stained fingers, it was obvious that serious business was being transacted. Not by one muscle spasm did my husband betray the hand that he was holding, but it was a 42 winning hand. Poker was his game, and in periods of financial difficulty he could always be relied upon to bring home an extra bob or two from a successful game. The fact that this kitty was never to be collected was one of the great miscarriages of justice in John's wartime memoirs, and the story was recounted many times.

The game was suddenly interrupted by a white-faced skipper who had been signalled by the wireless operator to proceed at all speed to a location far outside the harbour limits. No Royal Navy Launch was anywhere in the area. Flying Officer Bowen was nonplussed; outside the harbour were our own minefields to negotiate, and a decision like that could endanger all their lives. However, an order was an order and war was war. The game was abandoned temporarily, but John knew the game and the kitty were his.

'Let go for'ard, let go aft!' came the order, and with the crew looking white and horrified, the launch went speeding out of the harbour, heading towards the choppy open sea and the line of mines bobbing about invisibly outside the harbour. It was at this point that they met trouble, and John wept many a salt tear into his beer at the retelling of it. The small craft was nimble enough to clear a half-hidden mine, but it blew up behind them, throwing several of the crew up into the air and down onto the deck again, where they must have sent prayers up to heaven to save them, for they all thought they were too young to die. By the sound of the splintered deck boards and other ominous noises, it became apparent that High Speed Launch 111 was not going to be able to proceed a foot further without bailing out operations, for the wet and very cold water was already pouring all over the engine.

It was a matter of 'All hands to the pumps!' and working hard enough for her to limp back to base. They gingerly made their way back through that part of the line of mines they had negotiated on the journey out. Only then did they sigh with relief. Sea-sickness and terror have some devastating effects and several of the lads did not make it to the cabin. Those who did (John amongst them) viewed the wreck of the fo'c's'le with such dismay that it made the urgency of their errand even more imperative. Later that night, with icy hands encircling my waist, he wailed into the bedclothes,

'My trump hand blown out of the porthole, not a bloody card in sight, and not a smell of the kitty anywhere!'

'Aah,' I said, trying to make suitable noises and wanting to protest about his cold hands.

You never saw such waves,' he ranted on, 'they were mountains high. We all almost died tonight.'

'I know the feeling,' I yawned, 'I'm about to labour uncomplainingly for the benefit of the next generation, I might die as well.'

'You won't die,' he scoffed, 'A little thing like giving birth.'

I giggled, and he drew closer to me, though still bemoaning the loss of the cards and the disappearance of the kitty.

Next day, top brass from London came down to view the Launch and to try to assess the damage. John was up early and away to the base, to learn the fate of their beloved boat. From the shaking of heads, the low tones and the grave faces, they all guessed that High Speed Launch 111 was beyond repair and would no doubt have to be broken up. John came back to the bedsitter looking miserable. I steered clear of the topic of the trump cards, I knew it was a sore point. Later that night, some of the crew called for him to go to the pub. He looked half apologetically at me, for he had already said that he had no wish to go out again that night.

'You don't want to come, do you, Pet, not in your condition?' The question already answered for me, I glared belligerently at all four faces framed in the doorway. They seemed to be appealing to me not to put any obstacles in the way. They had 'men's business' to discuss.

Yes, I thought angrily, like the card kitty, or the possibility of a posting now that they were deprived of their precious speed boat. Besides, I was smarting a bit about the way John had added a comment about my 'condition'. He made it sound as though it was some kind of infection. If it had been, I thought viciously, I would have insisted upon going just to infect them all.

I gave a sigh of resignation.

'Don't be late,' was all I said, but the relief on all those faces made me turn aside to smile. They all trooped through the front door like schoolboys being let out to play. After they had gone, I read for a while, then pulled down the bed and was soon asleep. I kept dreaming of climbing a mountain but it was a long way right up there to the top. I was so weary and so tired.

'I can't go on,' I began to wail, 'It's no good, I can't go on.'

Then it seemed that a great crack appeared in the mountain side and I was falling down and down into its black depths. When I finally arrived at the bottom and looked up, I could see just a chink of blue sky which filled me with such joy and relief, that I knew I must strive with all my might to reach the top once more. Please God, I prayed, let me see the light again. I floated instantly and effortlessly to the top. The Mountain was still as high as ever, but I was near to God's sky, and not buried in that black hole. When I awoke the next morning, I felt strangely refreshed and less tired. I even sang a little tune as I scrambled over John to get to the kitchen to make tea. John was sitting up in bed when I returned to the room. He was holding his head and repeating his famous last words,

'Never again, oh, never again. Why did you let me go? I should have stayed home with you, Pet.'

From this I gathered that his night had been a good one and only his conscience bothered him a little this morning. He could shed that quite easily if only I would assure him that he had been right to go and leave me to sleep. I was not going to let him off that easily.

'Tea,' I said firmly, and set the cup on the arm of the settee.

Later that morning, Sgt Brodie called round to the house. John was shaving and his face was still covered in lather when I showed Brodie into the drab little room.

'Posting's come through,' he said, 'You and Smith are to proceed to Southampton on Friday. You will be kitted out there for a Posting to Gibraltar.'

He hardly glanced my way and only just managed a nod of recognition as he made his apologies and went out again. John saw him to the door. The lather was still on his face. I heard them talking for a while and when he returned to the room he looked anxiously at me as though once more it was him that needed to be assured that I would be alright. He wiped his face and then came over to where I was standing looking out of the window. He put his arms around me and whispered,

'I'm sorry, Pet,' like a small boy who has done something wrong and needs Mother to kiss him so that he can go out happily to play again.

I remained passively in the circle of his arms and made no attempt to give that kiss. I was eight months pregnant, scared and frightened but not wanting to let him know. I waited to hear him utter the same old remarks that I had heard before:

'You'll be alright, Pet. You're strong. You'll get by.'

When the words finally did come I muttered,

'Of course I will,' with an enforced enthusiasm that I did not feel, and disengaged myself from his arms. He was already whistling as he pulled out his kitbag and began to pack.

11 · *An Orange Juice Cocktail*

March came in like the proverbial lion with high winds that blew slates off roofs, and dust bin lids and debris everywhere. I struggled to the clinic holding on to my hat

John (standing at right) with some crewmates in 1940

with one hand, and clutching at a wool scarf wrapped around my neck with the other. The cold wayward wind played with the fringed edges, threatening to loosen the scarf from my neck, so that in the end I tied the woollie around my head and under my chin.

The clinic confirmed that all was well and they hoped to see me quite soon. They had given me the seventh of March as the approximate date of the baby's arrival. That day came and went. I was now feeling tearful and distressed. As I sat with Margaret in the big wooden armchair by the fire, she tried to joke to cheer me up.

'Lass,' she confided, coming close to me, 'a dollop of liquid paraffin and orange juice sometimes does wonders to shift a lazy babe.'

'I'd take anything to get started,' I wailed, for I was fed up with nothing happening.

51

I wasn't very big, and Margaret would often laugh and say she wondered what exactly I was covering up under my pinny.

'You don't eat enough to keep a cat alive,' she would say.

She now sent the two boys outside to play, then took a huge bottle of a greasy colourless mixture from a shelf in the cupboard and giggled as she poured out at least half a tumbler full. I remarked drily as she stood there measuring it that I reckoned it would have a better effect on her old squeaky treadle sewing machine than me.

'If this doesn't work then only a dose of gunpowder will,' she promised, and began to top up the revolting mixture with orange juice.

'Get it down you,' she said with mock severity, 'it has been known to act immediately.'

I looked at the glass and balked. Just a sip of it would make me sick. I thought of my misery and decided I couldn't stand that a moment longer. I took a deep breath and swallowed the lot. I was surprised that the orange juice was all I tasted, the rest slipping easily down my throat without my noticing it. I handed Margaret back the glass.

'I'll have another one of those,' I teased, 'and you can make it a double.'

'Get yourself home as fast as you can,' she urged me, and she was serious now. 'I'd come with you but I can't leave the boys.'

She kissed me and waved to me all the way down the street. When I went from the warm room of her house into the cold, I shivered and it was like cold water running down my back. I sneezed several times. God, I thought, not a cold to contend with as well.

When I got home I filled a hot water bottle and crept into bed. I felt slightly feverish and my dreams were broken and troubled. I woke myself up, groaning a little, and then became aware that some kind of rhythmic pain had awakened me. The clock told me that it was only 8:30

52

in the evening and I would have to get myself over to the pub to get the landlord to phone the ambulance for me.

My head swam a little when I stood up, my neck and back ached and something strange was happening in the lower region of my stomach. I thought grimly,

'Seems as though Margaret's jollop worked after all.'

The landlord of the Rising Sun took one look at my white screwed up face and assured me that he would have the ambulance at the door quicker than you could say 'Mine's a pint!'

He was as good as his word. Within 15 minutes, I was in the vehicle with two young attendants who sat holding my hand and whispering to me that,

'Everything will be alright, ducks, you'll be there in two shakes of a lamb's tail.'

Judging by the anxious looks on their faces, I think they were quite relieved when the Nunsthorpe Nursing Home came into view. I had a feeling they hoped that the part of their training involving a birth in their ambulance would never be put into practice.

At Reception, I was handed over to a very efficient uniformed nurse who took my particulars, plus my white admittance card. She relieved me of the small case I was carrying, and I followed her. I found myself in a tiny white cubicle. I was instructed to undress and get into a bath, but my troubles really began when, after the bath, they decided to give me an enema, which didn't help the effects of the jollop that Margaret had given me.

I was finally admitted to Labour Ward Four. As I staggered through the door of this clinically white, brightly lit torture chamber, I vaguely wondered if other young mothers felt that all the books about happy child-birth had been not quite true. All I was sure about at that moment in my ordeal was the quiet conviction that when Johnny came marching home again after one of his pub crawling sessions, uttering his usual 'Never again, never again!', I could echo that statement with 'Amen to that, dear!'

In the corner of the room was a kind of surgical trolley onto which I was ordered to climb. I was not very good at acrobatics and thought they must be joking. However, I was an obedient little soul and always tried to do my best to comply with authority, so I shoved one leg up onto the contraption, hoping for a helpful 'leg-up' from behind. No help came; instead a pain that made me hold my breath and grasp the steel bar of the trolley and which kept me in this position for several minutes. 'Ooooh', I mouthed, biting my lips and wishing I could tear my hair out at the same time. The squat little sister waddled over to where I was standing, still with one leg on the trolley, and demanded to know what I was making all the fuss about.

'You've had the sweet, now you must have the sour!' she said vindictively, and gave me a shove up on to the bed so hard that I arrived face down on a hard cold surface with just one pillow and nothing but a cold sheet to cover me. After a cursory examination that must have told them I would be in that stage of labour for some time, the Sister and the two nurses waddled out of the room and I saw them disappearing into the corridor outside. The sounds of babies crying in a nursery nearby came to me, and there were sudden little bursts of activity and laughter as footsteps hurriedly passed by Delivery Room Four, where I lay trying to cope with rhythmic contractions that seemed to come all too frequently now, with hardly any respite in between. Towards morning, I saw the grey dawn break.

I don't know how long I had been there on that cold trolley, but I knew when the contractions became urgent and different that somebody should be around. I tried to call out but all I could do now was to make horrible noises like some frenzied animal and grapple with a pain that threatened to squeeze the heart out of me. Then, without warning, a voice called out,

'Are you alright, how long have you been in here?'

Footsteps echoed in the corridor, mingled with the

sounds of frantic activity. I was being told to 'push'. I thought, 'I can't do much else.'

At 8:30 on March 15th, 1941, I gave birth to a baby girl. She was born twenty-two inches long and weighed barely five pounds. She gave one agonised little wail and went to sleep. I guess her journey into the world was not exactly a joyride and sleep was her only way to recover. As for me, I was glad when they wrapped me in warm red blankets and placed two hot water bottles on either side of me, wheeled me into a ward and put me into a bed.

I too wanted only sleep. Before I closed my eyes, I felt happy that I had my baby girl; Patricia Joy was the name I had already chosen for her. I turned my head towards the window and saw a big bush of yellow forsythia in bloom. I sighed contentedly and drifted off to sleep.

12 · *Motherhood*

I awoke the next morning to the sound of a trolley being wheeled along the ward and a cheerful voice calling,

'Cup of tea, ducks?'

I eased myself up in the bed to take the tea from the fresh-faced smiling young girl and made a wry grimace, for I felt as if I had been run over by a steam roller. Every part of me was stiff and sore. I sipped the tea with distaste — even that was lukewarm. I hated lukewarm tea. I slipped under the covers once more, but not for long. Sounds of bed-pans and running water added to the general hustle and bustle and conveyed to me that the daily routine of the Nursing Home was beginning. An hour later I was washed, toileted and had been fed. The breakfast consisted of cold lumpy porridge, thin burnt toast that tasted like charcoal, and a spoonful of pale anaemic scrambled egg which had been made from dried powder. I lost my appetite; cold food coupled with the strong smell of antiseptic and floor polish was not a combination likely to encourage one's taste buds. Like the Bisto kids, I loved my food, but I liked it hot.

Looking round the ward, where every bed with its neatly enveloped bottom was in line with its neighbour, I noticed an air of expectancy from all the bright-eyed and eager new mothers, who were now sitting up in bed arrayed in bright colourful nighties and crisp new bed-jackets. I snuggled closer into my warm flannelette night-dress, which was long enough to wrap my feet in if they were cold.

In the next bed to mine was a huge woman who was a bit of a celebrity. She had given birth, at the age of forty, to a bonny, bouncing ten pound baby boy. When I first caught sight of her, she was kneeling up in the bed, trying to retrieve some misplaced article from her bedclothes. I thought that she represented one of those fat little goddesses of fertility, probably called something roman-tic like Astarté, that the farmers used to worship in olden times. The richer the farmer, the bigger and fatter was the stone figure of Astarté. She had enough milk in those swinging udders to be surrogate mother to all the babies in the ward. She had long, straight greasy black hair and her rough voice whined when she timidly asked for anything. The Matron, along with all the nurses, thought that she was wonderful, the embodiment of mother-hood, and at the amazing age of forty years.

It was now time for all the infants to be fed. Sister Blood charged into the room. She was squat and fat and looked like a ship in full sail. From the vantage point of the first bed in the ward, I gave a little giggle and imagined her bellowing the order,

'Stand by your beds, girls. Mothers, bare your breasts and commence feeding your infants!'

The best and worst was yet to come. Matron led the way with the nurses in full attendance round her. They each held two infants, one in each arm, firmly bundled round in a tight papoose style. These they promptly distributed to all the fond mothers now sitting bolt upright in bed, ready to do their proud duty to their offspring.

'Let guzzling commence!' I thought grimly, and gritted my teeth.

Now it was my turn to see my little specimen and to rouse myself from the comfort of the bedclothes to do my bit. Sister advanced to our beds with the last two babies in her arms. Ten pound Billy Buster in the bed next to mine already looked about six months old. His wide blue orbs took in everything and when he was hurriedly slipped into his mother's waiting arms, she cooed and clucked, while he grunted like a large suckling pig. Her little treasure made immediately for the teat and began to gulp away with two chubby, tiny fists on both sides of this great appendage. He only stopped to burp and then went on sucking madly away. Meanwhile, on Sister's other arm was a small scrap of humanity, still asleep and taking no notice of the proceedings whatsoever.

'You will need to fatten this baby up,' Sister said with a disapproving look in my direction, 'Matron won't let her leave until she is five pounds in weight at least.'

I stole a look at my boobs and compared them with Astarté's milk bank in the next bed and wished I could sling my infant into the crook of her left arm. Even with the throbbing reminder that some milk was trying to filter through, they still only resembled a slight rising like two fried eggs. More humiliation was to come, because as I sat there eyeing this neat little bundle which looked like nothing so much as a small parcel which had just been delivered, Sister Blood sat down on the bed, whisked the baby up and pushed her small face into the region where my nipple should have been. She tried it from all angles, even pushing the tiny mouth under my armpit.

'Inverted nipples!' she roared, and the whole ward looked up, hearing the note of disapproval in her voice.

Patricia's lips shut tight. A stubborn streak plainly indicated that this was definitely not her favourite can of milk. She went back to sleep.

Sister Blood again strode into the ward, this time triumphantly bearing a white glass teat. Again the infant's head was pushed into the teat in a vain attempt to encourage the sad little nipple to rise from its crumpled state long enough for my babe to get the hang of it. Neither babe nor nipple responded. While Sister Blood fumed and I howled, the ward looked on amused and I was left in no doubt whatsoever that I was a pitiful failure. I suppose I should have been grateful to Astarté, for in the end she did supplement my milk. Sister Blood lived up to her name. She was after my blood and took a kind of fiendish delight in putting me through the torture of manually expressing my milk. At the end of one of these sessions she would eye the miserable couple of ounces of watery liquid with contempt and with a disdainful sniff, sweep from the room leaving me feeling battered and bruised, with only one word to describe Motherhood.

'Yuk!'

13 · Rolled Oats and Cow's Milk

During the whole time I was at the Nursing Home, I had but one visitor. When I looked up and saw Margaret, her cheeky face wreathed in a wide grin, coming down the ward, my spirits soared immediately and I spent the entire visiting period alternately giggling and coughing at the funny things she said.

'It ain't the coughing that carries you off, but the coffin they carry you off in!' was her dry rejoinder after one of my severe spasms had left me white and breathless. She opened the locker by the side of my bed, looking for a container for the small bunch of violets she had brought for me, and pounced triumphantly on a fish paste jar. She screwed up her nose in disgust when she discovered a thick layer of mould settled on the remains in the bottom, and disappeared down the corridor. When she returned, she had the jar washed and filled with water and placed the violets on the locker beside me. They were such a heavenly blue colour, I pressed my face into them. They reminded me of the dark cool places in the woods where we went when we were kids. It's funny how the fragrance of flowers lingers like memories.

Matron had been concerned about my cough as well. When later the next day she came and sat on my bed, she was careful t explain that she wished it was possible for her to allow me to stay for a few more days, but the beds were urgently required.

'Is there anyone at home to look after you?' she asked, anxiously, and looked relieved but not wholly convinced when I assured her that I would be alright.

'See the doctor about that dreadful cough,' she said, 'and as soon as possible get to the clinic for the free National Dried Milk. I doubt if you are going to be able to feed this lass of yours.' She leaned forward to touch my arm and pressed it reassuringly, and continued kindly,

'Persevere, though, my dear. You will find it so much more rewarding.'

The following morning, standing on the windswept steps of the Nursing home, waiting for the taxi to take me home, Matron handed me my baby wrapped up snugly in the shawl that I had so painstakingly made for her, then she pulled up the collar of my coat and walked with me down the flight of steps to where the cab had pulled up. As I waved her goodbye, I felt a slight pang of regret that now I was really on my own and realised I would miss the familiar though dull routine of the ward. From now on there would be no nursing staff to wait on me or to take the baby at night, to bath it and change it. Those duties would be mine. I leaned back further in the taxi so that my rib cage was clear of the arm rest separating the two seats, because the pressure hurt my side. We were speeding along the countryside, skirting the town now, soon we would be heading for the Dock area and Mill Lane. I screwed up my face. After the quiet of the Nursing Home, with its delightful surroundings, Mill Lane was not an ideal spot to dwell on.

The taxi was manoeuvring the maze of streets and finally turning into the lane and drawing into the kerb outside the house which looked even more depressing than usual. On this blustery March day, the smell from the gasometer was worse than ever, and as I opened my bag to pay the driver, I saw him wrinkle up his nose in disgust. He quickly reversed onto the dirt track by the side of the house and vanished within seconds. I sighed and inserted the key into the lock. Carrying the case and my baby, I found this simple feat alarmingly complicated, and was glad to reach the dark hallway and shabby stairway, where Robbie was now almost half way down, her laboured breathing loud and rasping. I set down the case and stood waiting for her to reach the last step. Her lovely grey eyes lit up when she saw Patricia, pulling aside the shawl to look at the sleeping elfin face.

'She's lovely,' she said at last, 'I could eat her.'

I sank down on the bottom stair with Robbie and sat for a while telling her all about the events of the week and making her laugh with the saga of Big Momma and Buster Billy in the next bed.

'The little 'uns get on just as well,' Robbie predicted. 'Just you wait, in a few weeks she will fill out. They say that this National Dried Milk blows 'em out — don't know what they put into it, but all the babies are right bonny.'

Robbie got up and went into the tiny kitchen to make me a cuppa, calling out to me that she had taken an extra pint of milk from the corner shop only that morning just in case I came home that day. I gave her the baby to hold and pulled down the bed. I placed a rubber sheet and a folded flannelette blanket on one side of the bed and, carefully removing the woollen shawl from her, I placed my precious bundle in the bed. I couldn't wait to crawl in beside her, for I felt so ill and ached all over.

'That's right,' Robbie commented, 'You get to bed, you don't look well at all, and a day's rest in bed will do you the power of good.'

I warmed up half the milk from the jug and poured it into a feeding bottle, then I wrapped it in the tea cosy and placed it under a pillow. Then, stiff and cold, I crept into bed and lay for several seconds shivering until the warmth from the blankets relaxed me and I fell asleep.

It was quite dark when I was awakened by Patricia making little threshing movements, her matchstick arms flaying the air. The sounds she made were like the faint mewing of a kitten. I guessed she was hungry, and hauled the bottle from its resting place under the pillow and tested the temperature of the milk by shaking a few drops onto the back of my hand. When I was satisfied that it was alright for her to drink, I heaved myself up on to my side and put the teat to her mouth. I knew instantly by the way she grabbed at it that she was in favour of this new arrangement, for in seconds she was drawing hard on the rubber and gulping away with relish. She didn't stop until a third of the bottle had been consumed, and was asleep again almost instantly. A slight burp was the only indication that she was filled and satisfied.

The next time I awoke was to see the sun through the partly opened green venetian blind, dancing on my bed. I lay there, not wishing to move because I felt so weary. I heard the sounds of the day's activity going on outside. A woman in the end house further up the street was talking to a passer by. Her rough loud voice carried along the street. The wind was still high, and from time to time blew in gusts, rattling the windows, and where the half panes were not locked, I could feel the cold blast of air on my face. I was too tired to get up to close the window. The baby was well below the bedclothes, so there was no fear of her being in a draught. After a while I drifted off to sleep again.

It was the morning of the third day that, when I awoke, I felt hungry. I knew this to be a good sign. When I put my feet to the cold lino, I shivered. The room was icy cold. Today I would have to light a fire and give Patricia her first bath. First I had to find something to eat because my tummy was making funny little rumbling sounds. I thrust my feet into some old slippers and pulled on a coat. Kneeling in front of the sideboard, I prayed fervently that I would find a box of shredded wheat. I could warm up the rest of the milk to pour over them. That would give me a fine substantial breakfast. Alas, there was nothing except a few handfuls of Quaker Oats at the bottom of a box, and in desperation, I stuffed them into my mouth, swilling them down with the remainder of the milk, which tasted slightly off, but I took no notice and finished the oats and the milk by tipping the box and allowing the rolled oats to trickle into my mouth from a corner. I was slightly breathless when I finished, but the hunger pangs had abated and I stayed there for several seconds before getting up slowly to make a pot of tea and to pinch a drop of Robbie's fresh milk.

Fortified and feeling much better now that I had eaten something, I set about raking out the grey dead ashes in the grate and, after a while, I had a bright fire going. I pulled up the dark green blinds so that the pale yellow shafts of the March sun shone through the window and filled the room with the promise of Spring. I glanced at my daughter, who was now wide awake, not making a sound but staring round the room, her big clear eyes taking in everything. I could have sworn she recognised me when I bent over to talk to her. She had been so good throughout those last three days, hardly moving or making a sound, but now I must give her a bath and freshen her up. I wondered how I would score on this, my first operation. When the bath was ready, and I had made sure that everything I would need was at hand, I went to the bed to lift her gently up and felt a wave of guilt when I discovered she was wet through right up her back. When her little body touched the warm water, she gave a little convulsive movement but soon relaxed and seemed to enjoy the soaping and the soaking. I was glad when the towelling stage was reached, as the bathing had been an ordeal for the both of us. Tomorrow it would come easier, I told myself, and laid Patricia on the bed to dress her. As I did so, I felt a flow of milk rush through my breast and trickle down my chest. I was so surprised. I guess it was all that resting in bed.

'No cold milk for you this morning, Miss,' I laughed, and held Patty close to me, trying to encourage her small button mouth to take a firm hold of that stupid little nipple. I knew that she favoured the bottle teat, but I prayed that just this once she might oblige me, because at that moment, I knew exactly how a dairy cow feels when it needs to be milked; I was very uncomfortable. She began to suck almost immediately, pulling with strong, swift gulps that seemed to stimulate nerves deep inside me. I felt the pressure go right through to my back, so that I winced with the pain of it. She lay there afterwards, just looking at me and I felt a strong surge of mother love rise up within me. I pulled her to me so that I felt the warmth and the sweetness of her.

'I'll make it up to you, Patty,' I said, 'I promise I will make it up to you.'

14 · *The Mauve Pram*

I started out to collect the pram that Margaret had promised me. She told me it wasn't up to much but it would keep the baby warm and dry and be a lot better than nothing. The baby was bathed and all ready, wrapped up in a warm shawl because, although it was April, the sky was grey and occasional flakes of white snow blew in my face. I was glad when I finally arrived at the row of neat little houses in Clyde Street. When I cuddled up in the big wooden armchair by her blazing fire, I thought back with nostalgia to the happy days I had spent with Margaret and wished that we were still neighbours. She made a fuss of the baby and said Pat was like me.

'Dead spit,' she predicted. 'Just you wait and see.'

The boys went wild with delight and instantly demanded that their mother have another baby, but not a 'sissy girl'. Margaret winked at me and bent down to whisper that having a baby meant that you make room for another one. I did not smile. I still held the view that babies should have the right to come into a home that was ready for them, along with an income that insured that they would be educated. In my mind a plan was already forming, and as soon as I was fit and well, I would carry it out.

'I'm going home, Margaret,' I said. 'As soon as I have saved the fare, I am going home.'

She didn't answer. Instead she told Tommy to get the pram out of the shed. Tommy looked at his Mother and cried out in protest.

'What! Give our pram away! What will you do if you have another baby?'

'Can't think about that till your Dad comes home,' she laughed and shooed him outside.

I went to stand idly by the door. I was unprepared for what I saw. As the pram finally emerged from the shed, very dusty and cobwebby, I blinked when I saw the colour of it. Margaret laughed aloud when she saw my face and with twinkling eyes told me that her husband had painted it a pale mauve when she had to use it for her second little 'un.

'A good clean up will work wonders,' she assured me. 'And the hood's not torn, neither is the apron. She'll be as snug as a bug in a rug.'

And the two boys thought that so funny that they giggled uncontrollably. There was a great deal of rubbing down and polishing. It was true that this pram would be better than humping the baby around in my arms. I did not have any money for a pram, and if I could have afforded the carriage of my dreams for this first lass of mine, it would have been a high Silver Cross carriage that I would have been so proud to have wheeled around.

The bottom end of the pram could be let down to make a pushchair. Two little silver clips kept that section of the pram in position and formed a deep well in the bottom of the pram when upright. Margaret informed me that it was great for holding all your groceries and would even take a bag of coal as well. I had a vision of myself in a cap and black shawl, taking a trip to the nearest pawn shop. I put the baby in the pram on a blanket that Margaret had found for me and pushed the pram out on to the pavement. I never did tell her that every time I man-oeuvred a kerbstone, I lost the babe when she slid down into this great well at the bottom of the pram.

This was the day I had to go to the clinic to have the baby weighed and to collect my two tins of National Dried Milk and free cod liver oil and orange juice. The hall was full of mothers and babies, and nurses busy placing infants in a weighing scoop and then entering each one's weight on to a card. There was a general hum of con-versation, young mothers excitedly discussing the new weight of their offspring with other mothers. Some were showing off the little darlings and discussing the latest knitting pattern and complicated stitch.

I was tired. I had pushed the pram a long way. I did not want to undress my baby. As yet, I had not got used to all the jerks and strange noises that came from her. I wanted only to collect the two tins of dried milk and be gone. Alas, a tall uniformed nurse curtly told me that I was very late and I might have to come back next week. She glanced at the small bundle in my arms and enquired if this was my first time. I nodded and was then told to undress the baby and to hurry and put her on the scales. Not feeling very pleased, I began the complicated task of extricating the matchstick arms from the clothing of my little fledgling. Ten minutes later, I was still there, trying desperately to avoid her slipping out of my arms and on to the floor. At home, I was getting used to handling her by placing her on the bed. The nurse standing impatiently beside me directed her remarks to the whole room. I was now the butt of their stares and amusement. She picked up the baby, and with a quick expert movement that any fool realised came only from handling a multitude of them, placed my baby on the cold weighing scales, whilst throwing me a scowl of disgust. Patty let out a howl of displeasure at the loss of her clothes and the coldness of the scales. At the same time, the nurse let out a stifled screech which turned every eye in our direction and made me go hot under my armpits.

'This baby, *this* baby,' she repeated, making her voice reach a high scale 'A', 'has not gained an ounce.' And turning to me she demanded in the same tone that struck terror into me,

'What have you been doing to this baby, *starving* her?'

There was an audible intake of breath as every pair of eyes now focussed on me. Even the knitting patterns were discarded. Here was a real live scandal. What self-respecting mother would want to starve her baby? What an unforgivable sin when the generous government was already doling out free National Dried Milk and orange juice and cod liver oil.

I saw the open hostility in their eyes and I was all set for flight. I had a hunted feeling and realised that this great institution could actually take my baby away from me. I removed the protesting scrap from the scales and began to dress her. I laid her on the floor where I knew she would be safe, and where best I could handle her. I was on my knees beside her, feeling my face red and tears very near. I ignored the nurse and her scathing remarks, and when I had finished dressing Patricia I wrapped the shawl very tightly round her and marched up to the tiny counter, where a young girl, leaning on her elbows,

66

was taking in the whole procedure. When she saw me coming, she withdrew her elbows and watched me with an insolent stare. No doubt I was already condemned in her opinion. Of all the articles that passed for mothers, I had no doubt, that afternoon I took the biscuit. I placed two blue round tokens on the counter and said in a clear, calm voice,

'Two tins of National Dried, please, and I will take the cod liver oil and the orange juice only if they are free.'

She again smirked, but said nothing, and slid the two tins of milk through the opening. Two bottles of cod liver oil came through next, but not the orange juice, which cost 10d; and after that she again put her elbows on the counter and surveyed me with the same insolent smirk. I grabbed my tins of milk, and feeling completely cowed, left with as much dignity as I could muster.

I walked to the bottom of the hall where I had left the pram right by the entrance. All the brand new prams were lined up against the wall in neat rows. Woollen pom-poms, beads and satin ribbons graced the fronts, and expensive eiderdowns and coloured blankets lay folded back waiting for the fortunate babies to be laid in them. The mauve monstrosity stood away from the rest. It looked more like a garden wheelbarrow than a pram-cum-pushchair. With my nose in the air, I put Patty in the thing and the dried milk in the well. It was true what Margaret had said — that a whole week's groceries could be stored in the bottom. I could even pick up a bag of coal on my way home.

The line of eyes that had followed my progress up to the counter had reversed whilst following me down the room. A silence had fallen and the hush had continued as their eyes followed me making for the hideous lilac-coloured pram. Nobody moved as I pushed open the door and the pram and I made our exit. Then a great burst of laughter, disturbing and mocking, came through an open window. I leaned over to hang on to Patty and prevent her from slipping into the bottom of the pram again as I let it down the kerb to cross the pavement, and then I ran as fast as my weary legs could carry me all along the road. When I was out of sight of the clinic, I stopped for breath, filled with humiliation and rage. Then, as now, anger compels me to make a move. I stood there white and shaken, and knew that it was only I who could make things change for me. Suddenly I was filled with a deep longing for Bristol and all that was dear and familiar.

'We are going home,' I whispered to Patty. 'You and I are going home.'

15 · *A New Green Dress*

I dropped my first two shillings towards the fare home into a chipped cup and set it resolutely away in a cupboard. I knew that I could not make an immediate flight, it would mean saving these few precious shillings each week for months yet. However, something was about to happen that forced me to leave very much sooner than I was prepared for.

I had not seen Robbie for some time. On the brief occasions when I saw her on the stairs or in the scullery, I would be bustling around to get me and Patty away from the Road and down to the beach or along the harbour wall. Today, we were going again into Cleethorpes with Margaret and the boys. Robbie's eyes had brightened when she saw Patty and she stopped to talk to her. I thought nothing of the unusual pallor of Robbie's white face or the blueness of the thin lips drawn so tightly in one thin line because of the difficulty of breathing. I had seen Robbie so many times gasping on the steps. Often she stayed in her bed all day, only emerging for brief periods to enquire where we had been that day and to view the progress of the baby with that bright smile of hers.

'By gum — that Government milk certainly blows 'em up,' she would laugh, and delightedly begin to tub Patricia's chubby thighs, who would chuckle back at Robbie and grab at the finger that Robbie held out to her.

She called to me that morning to have a good day and she came to the door to wave as we went off down the street. From one of the houses came the strains of Vera Lynn, a wireless blaring out that favourite forces song.

We'll meet again,
Don't know where, don't know when,
But I know we'll meet again
Some sunny day . . .

I had heard from John, who was now in Gibraltar. His letter contained a description of the place. There was really just one main street, with shops and traders who only wanted your money. The Spanish borders were patrolled day and night and kept out of bounds to all servicemen and there was little to do except defend this gate to the 'Med', lounge on the beach and drink beer. He enclosed a snap of himself doing just that, sunbathing in shorts, sitting at a table under a huge beach umbrella with a glass of beer in his hand. The letter ended with a request for books because these were difficult to get. He hoped that I was well and that I would write soon to let him know if he was the father of a son.

Now I had an address, I could write. It was six weeks since I had seen John and he had become a vague figure standing somewhere in the background. Like so many other women in those war years, I had to carry on alone; the whole burden of bringing up the children fell on us. I wrote to tell him that a baby girl was now very much alive and kicking, called Patricia Joy. I hoped that he would approve, both of the baby girl and the name I had given her.

I arrived at Margaret's. She excitedly told me that Tom Bradley, my former landlord, had acquired a whole roll of material on the Black Market and was letting it go dirt cheap for three bob a yard. I was full of interest. Margaret had told me many a time that she would always run up a dress for me on that treadle machine of hers. She wasn't very good at knitting, but she was a wizard on the machine. I could do with a new dress — but — and here I thought of that little cracked cup which held the cash to enable me to get home.

'It's the most beautiful moss green jersey you ever saw,' she tantalised, 'I can get you a length if you just say the word.' I hesitated.

The next moment she was showing me a pattern that she insisted would be just right for me. I capitulated and urged her to get it for me as soon as possible.

The next few days found us busy laying out the pattern onto the material that she slipped over to Tom Bradley's to get, and I had raided the chipped cup with a slight feeling of guilt, knowing that such extravagance would set me three weeks back from my goal. Still, I argued, it would help to make the waiting that bit more bearable. As Margaret snipped away with the scissors, I could almost see myself in that finished dress. It was going to be cut on a princess flare with a Peter Pan collar and cuffs, and buttons all the way down the front. I would buy a cord tasselled belt and daringly leave the bottom button undone.

'Brazen hussy,' Margaret laughed, with her mouth full of pins. 'You'll have all the old men falling off their bikes looking round at you.'

I couldn't wait for the dress to be finished.

The house was strangely quiet when I entered it that night, and I became aware that I hadn't seen or heard Robbie for the past few days. I called up the stairs to ask if she would like a cup of tea but there was no answer and I suddenly became alarmed. It had only been a week ago that the old lady in the front room had fallen in the scullery and broken her arm. She had been taken to the hospital but no relatives had been to see her. Robbie had commented on how she had missed the dear old soul and hoped she would be alright. It was not only the sombre silence of the house that alarmed me, but something else that made me race up the stairs two at a time to pound on Robbie's door. It was a kind of inward knowledge that I had seen her wistful lovely smile for the last time when she had followed me to the gate and waved to me.

Why oh why hadn't I shown Robbie the same concern — why hadn't I called out last night to see if she was alright? My mind had been too full of that damned dress — so eager was I to sit by Margaret and to watch the material speeding under that needle and those active hands of hers transforming the length of soft green jersey into a dress that would be exciting to wear. Having that dress meant so much to me: a kind of reward now the long months of pregnancy were over, and I wanted to feel attractive again. After the birth of Patricia, there had been no one to come home to, there had been no cuddles, no one to make a fuss of me and the baby. Just the two of us in that cold little room with no one to confide to that I was scared as hell with the weight of responsibility of a baby, and feeling so ill. When Margaret finally purchased that length of material from Tom Bradley, I had come home and daydreamed about the finished dress. I saw myself swinging easily and confidently down the road with those two bottom buttons undone, the gold braid belt with the tassels tied loosely at the side, bare legs in white sandals, giving a toss of my dark curls to all the women staring so enviously at me. Well, even if none of those extra things happened, and I knew that they would not, it was good to dream about. It made me feel better somehow, a good old fantasy dream helped all the mundane things in life and life was eighty percent mundane things.

Now I paused with my hand on the handle of the door, wanting to hear Robbie's voice calling breathlessly for me to enter and to see her eyes light up when I began to tell her about the saga of the day. I always made her laugh when I exaggerated and embroidered the trivial little

71

happenings and altered my voice to mimic pompous and authoritarian characters who opposed me.

When I pushed open the door, I knew instantly by the deathly silence in that shadowy room that Robbie was no longer there. Something that resembled her lay propped back against the pillows, her half closed eyes now focused on something beyond any mortal scene. Her mouth had fallen slightly open as though caught unawares in one of those painful intakes of breath she had borne uncomplainingly in life.

'Oh Robbie,' I said, and the tears that fell were tears of self pity because she was such a gentle soul and I loved her so. Now, never again would I see her grey eyes light up with pleasure and her face soften when she saw Patricia.

'Why, oh why,' I sobbed, 'Do all the people I love have to vanish suddenly and go away? And why couldn't I have checked that she was alright the night before?'

God, how awful to die alone. Nobody should have to do that. It was all my fault.

After a while, feeling spent and empty, I made my way down the stairs and across the road to sob out my sad little story to the landlord of The Rising Sun. I leaned heavily upon this plump genial man in moments of stress, and I never did pay him for all the phone calls he made on my behalf.

'Nay lass,' he said when I had given him the sad message, 'don't take on so. 'Twas none of your making and folks round here all knew about her heart condition. She was a brave and lovely lady.'

I could only nod miserably and cry some more.

He sent for the ambulance and also for Robbie's sister, who lived at Loughborough. The ambulance men came and took Robbie away wrapped in a white sheet. Robbie's sister came the following day. She was as plump and stout as Robbie had been thin and tall. She had none of the gentleness and humility of her sister; she was business-like and very efficient.

'The house is unsafe,' she said with finality, 'and I have no wish to continue with the letting of it. No doubt it will be earmarked for demolition. Despite all our pleading and attempts to get her to give up this house and come and live with me, she insisted on remaining here on this awful bomb site. And all because she said she wanted to be independent. Sheer lunacy I call it!'

She made this last statement with such scorn, as though being a spinster and independence should not go together.

'Not all women choose marriage,' I said. 'Because Robbie chose another road you should not be contemptuous of her. I think she was a very brave person.'

She did not pursue this line of argument, but it was obvious that she was not in sympathy with it.

'I have a limited time in which to settle my sister's affairs,' she said imperiously, 'I have to be back in Loughborough by next week. Shall you be happy with a week's notice, then? I am sorry it is all at such short notice, but you see how it is."

I wheeled Patty round to Margaret's on the day of Robbie's funeral. She had offered to look after her in order that I could attend the service at the tiny church on the edge of town. There was just Robbie's sister and myself that day. I looked up at the high dome of the building and wondered why all churches are built so lofty and seem so cold, aloof and intimidating. Maybe the feeling of being so small and insignificant was deliberate, and brought home the fact that it is only our egos that make us believe we are bigger than we are; here in this awesome place we can dance nearer to the flame of reality. I thought about birth and death.

'I do not know what came before,' I pondered, 'and do not care much for what comes afterwards. All that is really important is the here and now.'

We sang Robbie's favourite hymn.

Oh love that will not let me go,
I rest my weary soul in thee,
I give thee back the life I owe,
That in its ocean depths, its flow may fuller, richer be.

73

Later, when the coffin was being lowered into the earth, I pulled a red rose from the wreath that her sister had sent and was now placed by the side of that gaping great hole. I threw the rose onto the shiny bright wooden casket and whispered, 'Goodbye, Robbie.'

If life was a series of stations along the way to some unknown destination, Robbie had come to the end of hers. Soon there would be another station for me to alight at. What changes would there be for me? I walked thoughtfully back for the last time to Mill Lane and the solitude of an empty house.

16 · *Going Home on a Wing and a Prayer*

A few days later, I stood on the platform of Grimsby Dock once more. I had been away from Bristol for almost two years. As I stood there, I recalled the foggy November night when I had first caught sight of John standing by the solitary light on this very platform. Was I the same girl who had run laughing from the carriage with that young soldier who had befriended me? The one who had run to that dark figure, full of excitement, waiting for two arms to reach out and hold her, assuring her that she had been wrong to have doubts?

I stood by the lamp alone now and that same young girl seemed to mock me from the shadows.

There was a queue for tickets, mostly soldiers going home on leave. I sat on a seat waiting for the line of servicemen to diminish. I was also waiting to pluck up courage to ask for a ticket I couldn't pay for. I had never quite saved up enough to get the fare together. The green dress had made such a hole in my cash, that I now regretted that last impulsive purchase. When the dress had been finished and pressed, Margaret took it herself to the shop a few streets away for the buttonholes to be done professionally. She had stepped back to view it when I finally tried it on and said with real pride in her voice,

'Ee lass, you look right bonny in that colour, with your dark hair and all.'

We hugged one another then and cried at the severance of our friendship. Our paths would never meet again.

I waited for a lull in the lines of people queueing for tickets and finally approached the ticket booth, but immediately a fresh queue formed behind me made up of both soldiers and civilians. My heart was beating so fast as the opening to the ticket box came nearer. The uniform-clad figure of the ticket clerk, his eyes intently fixed on his job of issuing small pieces of cardboard, did not even look up as he automatically called out,

'Next please!' and I hesitated before blurting out,

'Please, I want to get to Temple Meads and I haven't got any money. But I promise I'll send the cash as soon as I arrive home, honestly I will!'

His head jerked up then, for the smooth running routine of the morning had been shattered by the voice of a chit of a girl that he couldn't even see properly. He peered over his glasses to get a proper look at me whilst I burst into tears with nervous agitation, and the people in the queue behind shuffled uncomfortably.

I was sobbing with the enormity of the nerve it had taken me to muster up the courage to ask for a ticket I had no money to pay for. My tears were genuine enough, for after the first shock of my desperate attempt I was filled with rage that I had been put to such lengths — so that it was self-pity that made the tears fall so readily.

The reaction to my tears was electric. A young soldier in the queue behind me fumbled for his wallet in the back pocket of his trousers and reached forward to thrust a folded note onto the paybox, whilst several people stepped sideways out of the line to see better what was going on.

75

The man in the ticket box coughed, then waved the back of his hand over the money as if to tell the young man that it would not be necessary, and motioned me to come round to the side entrance. The young man picked up his cash and accompanied me to the door of this tiny room. Seated in a swivel chair by a table strewn with timetables and other station paraphernalia, and filled with abject misery, I snivelled loud and long. The soldier handed me his handkerchief whilst the man in front of the window did his best to reduce the line of enquiring faces who insisted on peering curiously into the tiny opening to stare at me and Patty. Someone brought me a cup of tea, which in normal circumstances I would have been grateful for. Now, severe hiccups prevented me from taking even a sip. The tea slopped into the saucer and mingled with my salt tears.

Finally, the dark blob of the ticket clerk turned away from the opening in the booth to where we were sitting and handed the young soldier a ticket for me. Pointing towards the train that had pulled up on the other side of the track, he instructed him to make sure that I was safely on it, because that was the train I would need. I allowed the young man to take Patricia from me. He did it so easily and effortlessly. He held her in the crook of his arm and with his free hand he piloted me, still hiccupping, over the bridge and onto the train, which was hissing and snorting to be away from the platform.

Once seated on the train, he sat there opposite me still holding Patty and watching me with deep concern. Then he reached into his pocket and brought out a flask. Handing it to me, he urged me take a sip.

'Go on,' he said, 'it will calm your nerves.'

I did as I was told and took a big sip. The brandy burned my throat and took my breath away so that I coughed and spluttered, but the hiccups vanished and I could feel a warm feeling spreading all over me. I thought hysterically of the other squaddie who had befriended me on that cold November night two years ago. Now

76

another soldier was also helping me and I wondered what John would have had to say about that.

'Can't take my eyes off you for one second,' I mimicked him in my mind.

When eventually the train began to move, I sat in the corner feeling embarrassed and degraded. I did not want to look at the young man. My poverty made me feel angry. I hated being at the mercy of other people's generosity, yet there he was, still holding my baby so naturally and silently giving me such support.

'We could have been husband and wife,' I thought, and felt my eyes sting with tears again.

Some twenty minutes later we reached a station and the soldier rose from his seat and gently returned Patricia to me.

'Will you be alright now?' His deep set eyes still showed his concern. On impulse I caught both his hands and held them to my face.

'Of course,' I said, 'and I shall be eternally grateful for what you've done for me today.'

He squeezed my hand, opened the door and was gone, swallowed up in a sea of nameless people. The carriage was now silent and empty, and how I wished he could have stayed.

At King's Cross, I collected my bits and pieces together and expertly pulled Patricia over onto my left hip so that I would have one hand free. I took out my purse containing the precious six shillings that I had managed to save and not surrender to the ticket man. I walked with confidence to the cab rank and calmly asked for my destination. The sixpenny tip I offered at the end of my journey was given with a slight smile, for I remembered that other taxi journey, and it earned me a half salute as the cab door was slammed shut behind me and it drove away.

More memories filled my mind as I neared familiar countryside and we finally hissed into Temple Meads station. It was 1941. What changes would I find here, and how would I be greeted, after an absence of almost two years? I alighted from the train and sat on a seat to extract my ticket from my purse. Patricia wriggled.

For several minutes I gave my attention to her as she noted the new sights and sensations with excited little gestures towards the train still hissing its great length along the platform.

'That, Patty,' I stated, 'is a TRAIN.' No baby talk for this infant, I had already decided. A horse would be a horse, and no 'gee-gee's' allowed.

Then I started to notice the bomb damage: the buffet and the waiting room were no longer there. I missed the friendly station that had housed all those seaside posters along with the bustle of porters struggling with great cases denoting holidays. All that was gone and in its place was a kind of austere politeness from the skeleton staff, almost like a quiet acceptance of what was lost.

My gaze swept along the train that was just moving out and suddenly thoughts unbidden leapt into my mind. So vivid was the impact that I felt a pang in my chest that was like a stab wound. I remembered Gord waving from the window as his train began to move slowly forward and snake round the bend. Once more I was on this very platform, with the face that I had loved leaning far out of the window calling,

'Write every day — promise?'

Then the bend in the rails had taken him out of sight and I had sat on this very seat struggling with emotion. Those letters that I had treasured so much had lessened in the months that followed, until they had dwindled to the occasional one. Somehow, I had guessed — knew, in fact, even before that final letter had arrived to tell me. His going home had renewed a friendship with a childhood sweetheart which both families had favoured and hoped for. Now Marion was pregnant and they were to be married. He hoped I would find someone fine and worthy of me but he said that though Marion needed him, I was strong and I would get by. A voice inside seemed to shout,

'Don't be bitter.'

I picked up Patty abruptly and made my way out through the station. I noticed that the clock and all the facade of Temple Meads had been damaged. At the bottom of the incline there had been a paint warehouse where a pile of rubble now stood. (I bet that had been a blaze!) I stopped several times on my way to the bus stop, to change the baby from one hip to another, because at four months she was getting heavy, and I had a long way to go. I stopped again on the bridge. A lot of water had flowed beneath that bridge since last I stood there. As I turned sharp right to walk along by the river and to point out to Patty the white swans, I saw the gaping hole in the church roof of St Peter's and stood gazing in abject misery at the devastation to my beloved Castle Street, now barricaded off because of the piles of rubble where it had almost been razed to the ground.

I had to retrace my steps and cross the bridge again, skirting Castle Street and coming out at the end of Tower Lane, and thus I entered Old Market, where before the war the tramcars and tram lines used to end on the cobblestones, and flower sellers and stalls piled high with fruit were crowded together every Saturday, and dogs barked and people laughed and carried home their bargains on the open decked trams.

No tram cars now; instead a solitary bus to Kingswood stood by the Shepherd's Hall. Greyhound Bus Service, it said all along its side, and I made my way to board the vehicle.

I prayed that nothing would have changed at Kingswood. That cold house at South Road called me and yet repelled me, and as yet I did not know why. I didn't know what kind of reception I would get. I hoped that my absence would have mellowed my mother, because I desperately wanted a relationship with her. I had heard from my mother only three times in those past two years. Certainly she had not wanted me to stay at home after my marriage. She too had wanted to be her own woman.

I understood that. Perhaps that would all be forgotten now that I was going home. I hoped she would be glad to see me, for where else would I stay if. . . I couldn't let my mind dwell on that possibility.

The bus laboured up Two Mile Hill and so far nothing had altered. When I alighted at Downend Road I saw the damaged Odeon Cinema. With apprehension I realized how near that had been to home. I slipped along Halls Road and down the lane, Jackson's Foundry and Jenkins' garden all still there. Then I had my hand on a new green gate with a black painted latch that you pulled down to open. I remembered the old one with its peeling paint and the dented brass handle with the loose spindle that Lady pulled at with her teeth so that the whole lot would fall on to the path with a clatter. It seemed in that instant as though Lady would come bounding out to greet me. Everything else was the same; the privy door right next to the back kitchen, and the tin bath still hanging on the wall by its huge six inch nail, but the middle room window and the top bedroom window were boarded up — bomb blast, no doubt, from the bomb that had fallen on the cinema at the top of Halls Road.

I opened the back door quietly. The old tap was still dripping and the great iron stove with its black band stood along the wall. The dresser was bare and pictures taken from the wall left spaces as sad reminders of their former friendly splendour. My mother was busy on her knees wrapping china in newspaper and her head was half hidden in the interior of the wooden packing case. She glanced up, startled at my quiet entry into the room, and peered through the semi-darkness to where I stood with Patricia in my arms. She stopped to look more closely as though she could hardly believe the evidence of her eyes.

'Our Joyce? What are you doing home?'

I came further into the room and sat on the arm of the old faded velvet chair. I was so tired and wanted so much to sleep once more in that whitewashed bedroom of mine and to wake up and not see all the change that I could not cope with — not today and not here.

My mother sighed, a deep sigh.

'Well, you have chosen a fine time to come home, my girl, another hour and we should have been gone. We're moving today.'

'Moving?' I repeated stupidly, 'Why? Where?'

'We've bought a business-'

She broke off suddenly to turn to my father who had just come in from the front room to say to him,

'Look what the wind has blown in — it's our Joyce.'

'Well, well, well,' was all Dad could say, but he came over to the baby now asleep in my arms. 'Nice little thing.' He continued to look at the baby, obviously at a loss to know what to do or say.

'Look,' he said at last,' we can't offer you a cup of tea, everything is packed, we are waiting for the van to arrive-'

'It's alright,' I now hastened to assure them, 'after I have seen Auntie Elsie and Bert, I am going to Gwen's. John's sister, you know, she is expecting me.'

The relief on both their faces made me smile. The lie that had come so glibly took me by surprise. I had expected many things but not this.

'Maybe when we are settled you could come and stay with us for a week or two,' my father was saying, looking towards my mother for confirmation of this last statement. It did not come. Again I had the impression of silent hostility that I had shown up at all.

'When we turned out the under-cupboard we found nothing but doll's arms and legs.' My mother was looking at me accusingly. 'That right, Dad?' She shot this question at my father who was now helping her to finish packing a last pile of plates.

'Ahh' was all he said and laughed at the recollection. 'All those lovely dolls your mother dressed for you and you pulled all their arms and legs off.'

'Hope you don't start pulling her limbs off in the same

way,' she shot at me. I stood back at the open hostility in her voice.

'There's one complete dolly left — you might like to have it for her,' said my father, and he went over to where a very dishevelled doll with matted hair lay propped in a corner.

'It still says 'Mama,'' he said, and turned the doll over so that a sad and pathetic little 'MaaMaa' came from it.

'I must go,' I said, for I wanted suddenly to run from the room. I knew at that instant that the enmity between my mother and me would always be there. The precious bond between us had been severed the day when I left as a child from that very room for Painswick. I had hoped that this bond could be replaced by a friendship between two women. But I could not stay in that house any longer. There was no need to. Every creak on the stairs would be etched on my memory forever.

I picked up the doll for Patty. It bent over as I did so and uttered again its mournful cry. From somewhere deep inside me I heard the cry re-echo like a great sob that took my breath away so that I could hardly speak.

'MaaMaa,' it wailed, 'MaaMaa.'

17 · *Nightingale Valley and Auntie Gwen*

The sun was just setting and the song of a blackbird in the bough of an old apple tree could be heard as we turned down the incline called Nightingale Valley to Gwen and Harry's cottage, situated right by the side of St Anne's station. Elsie and Bert had insisted on driving me over to Brislington in their little Jowett car and stayed long enough to hear Gwen declare that she wouldn't hear of us staying anywhere else but with them.

Joyce with John's mother, Minnie, and sister, Gwen, outside Gwen
and Harry's cottage

'It's the very least I can do for my brother and his wife.
Looking after Patty will be my contribution to the war
effort and Joyce can go to work if she wants to.'

Elsie and Bert made me promise to visit them now that
I was back in Bristol again. Bert came often to the Valley
just to pick Pat up and take her over to see his mother at
Barton Hill.

Oak Cottage was one of a pair that stood squarely
facing up the valley so that directly you turned into the
terrace, the cottages with their gardens full of flowers
were the first things you saw. On one side there were
woods and fields and at the bottom of a steep bank on
the other side there ran the main railway line from
Temple Meads through to Bath with the tiny halt of St
Anne's. On the other side of the railway and over the

bridge was an avenue of bungalows and fine houses with mature trees that graced the gardens and lined the entire length of road. Over the whole area lay a languid peace and tranquillity. It seemed as though this sacred spot had been deliberately passed over by any wind of change and no scar of war touched or marred it. The two years that Patty and I were there brought joy and pleasure to both of us, as well as a kind of healing balm that helped to eradicate the trauma of those months at Grimsby.

Harry reminded me of a pilgrim father. When he had occasion to chastise his small brood of two boys and one girl, he would look very grim and stern as they stood in front of him and he delivered his lecture. After they had been dismissed, I would detect a light chuckle, but he would always turn aside so that the tell-tale smile did not show. I suspected he was a softie at heart. However, he was firm and just, and his children accepted the telling off knowing it was justified. Gwen never interfered with her husband's authority as head of the household and if the running of it was slightly Victorian, I could not oppose it, for here in this cottage I found a sense of stability that I never found in that cold loveless house at South Road. A tin of sweets was kept on the top shelf, as a reward for jobs well done. Nobody could dig to the bottom for favourites; you took from the top or went without. Nobody questioned this golden rule.

Gwen and Harry called each other 'Dear'. Harry, as the head of the house, came first and was served first, then came the children in order and Gwen always put herself last. My forthright views were dismissed with a sniff from Gwen,

'Joyce is on her soapbox again!'

Gwen held to one moral judgement, that 'right was right and wrong was no man's right'.

Gwen was happy and even-tempered. I never heard her shout or raise her voice. Flustered maybe, and indignant yes, but for the space that two more people took up in that small two-up-and-two-down, not one grouse or grumble did she ever utter. I shall always be grateful to those two people for the love they extended to me and Pat.

At 5:30 each evening, Gwen would take Pat to meet Harry from work. He was a railwayman and worked on the station right by the side of the house. Patty had a special hug and kiss. Uncle Harry was a firm favourite. When he was locked away in his shed she knew he was making her something special which was a secret and he wasn't to be disturbed. He made all the children's toys when they were young: a toy duck that bobbed up and down when she pulled it along on a string, and a wooden clown that actually jumped right over a bar when you squeezed both sides together, a wooden cot and real blankets that Auntie Gwen had made for her, and now he was making her a small trolley — there was no end of things that you could carry around in that. Patty loved Auntie Gwen and Uncle Harry. A new tooth, first steps, and first words were a celebration for the whole family. Sometimes I felt a pang of sadness that my own mother was not any part of this domestic scene, but I took heart in the fact that these simple but precious things were valued in this family and I felt proud and important because of it.

I went to work at the Magna Products at Warmley, a big engineering firm with huge war-time contracts. My first impression of this great all male domain was not a good one, and the dust, grit and grime mingled with a strong smell of oil, along with all the lathes and machinery, awed and scared me. Because of the shortage of men, women were coming into the foundries and into the Works. There were women conductors on the buses taking over until the men came home again, though, at the end of the war, they were not so keen to let go of their new independence. The end of this war brought many unheard and undreamt of changes.

I was introduced to a great monster called a milling machine. A press of a button set the thing in motion and a huge saw cut slots in round chunks of metal. A trickle of milky white liquid played onto the saw and it was part of my job to ensure that this lubricating fluid was always kept running, otherwise the saw would buckle with the heat of the revolutions. The price of a new saw was pretty high. Anyway, I became proficient at handling this machine and so they gave me two to run. As one machine stopped, the other was set in motion. From time to time, a white coated Inspector would come around with a micrometer to make sure that the slots were exactly the right size. This was extremely important as they had to be milled to a thousandth of an inch. Apart from the boredom of merely walking up and down to start and stop these great things, there was little else to do, although I was thrilled and proud to learn that it was my two milling machines that helped to make the bonus for the whole shop. With the extra money in my pay packet, I was able to save more and have money to give to Gwen for my keep and to buy Patty pretty dresses.

When the sirens sounded, it was works policy to leave the factory and file quickly into the shelters. One day, a bomb made a direct hit on one of the shelters at the Filton Aerodrome works, killing all the people inside. Later that day, all the other employees at Filton had been sent home because of the tragedy. They had arrived home white and shaken, none of them being able coherently to tell the story, and wondering how their friends and workmates could ever be properly buried. The shelters at Filton were never re-opened, but were sealed over and became a tomb.

After that, we were not so inclined to use the shelters at our works but would get right away from the place and run into the fields instead. Some of the men would make a bee-line for the pubs if they were open, but I enjoyed fresh air and the break from the dusty atmosphere of the machine shop. It cleared my head so that I was more alert when I returned.

One morning on Day Shift and just about to clock on,

I saw my father in the queue ahead of me and called out to him. His face lit up when he saw me, he was so pleased that he walked me all the way to the foundry and insisted on introducing me to his foreman and the rest of the men already there. He said that because of the war they could not get the young lads to make the cores for the moulds, but now they had women to do the work. He looked down at the floor before admitting that they were far better at it than any of the men, with many fewer 'wasters'. I noted that he was careful not to use the word that was foundry slang, which was 'shitters'. I smiled now when I remembered how my mother always told him off when he used the word at home.

'How is everything?' I blurted out suddenly, for I was anxious to know how Dad came to be at the Magna Products, since the last time I had seen him he was so full of going into a business with Mum. Again he looked uncomfortable. He shuffled his feet and cleared his throat. My directness always disconcerted him and having to be disloyal made him uneasy.

'Not enough for both of us to do in the shop,' he said gruffly, 'and your mother is a better business head than I shall ever be. This is what I am better at.' He spread his hand expansively around the foundry. 'She is happy doing what she is doing back there.'

His head jerked backwards, indicating some obscure location that he hoped I wouldn't probe into, but this hesitancy of his only made me more insistent so that my next question made him look even more flustered than before.

'Where is this shop of yours, then?'

'At Ashley Hill.' His answer was evasive and came much too quickly. Like a bloodhound, I was on the scent and was not going to be put off now.

'Whereabouts in Ashley Hill?' I stared hard at Dad so that he had no option but to meet my gaze.

'Half way up the hill,' he said reluctantly, and I was suddenly very angry that it had been necessary to have

87

almost to drag this information out of him. It was as though I was the black sheep of the family. Like some revelation, it became clear to me that there must be some other reason for Dad's disinclination to disclose their present whereabouts. I met my Father's eyes in an attempt to compel him to be honest with me so that we could both get back on the same footing we had shared when I was a small girl, but he shifted his gaze to the floor and refused to look at me. In that instant, I knew for certain that he was remembering a night, some years back, on which something had happened that had caused him so much pain, and for which, because he could not blame my mother, he was shifting the guilt on to me.

'Dad,' I said and moved towards him. I wanted to plead with him that this alienation was more than I could bear, and talking about it might ease the situation even if it didn't solve anything. The look of pleading in his eyes cut short the torrent of words that threatened to spill out.

'No — don't say anything.' His voice came in dull, flat tones and he stared into space. 'I blame you, Joyce, for what happened. You were there and knew what was going on. You should have told me.'

Well, it was out now; another load of guilt to carry on my back. I was glad at that moment to hear the shrill clanging of the Works bell, a summons for commencement of the day's round and common tasks. Dad still stood motionless, his hand thrust deep inside his pockets and staring hard at the floor. His face wore the look of a man tormented, and the hardness gave the impression that he was incredibly old. I knew I would never penetrate that formidable wall of resistance, and I walked away and left him standing there. As I walked slowly back to the machine shop, I had a sudden mental vision of South Road. The house pulled yet repelled me. It was as though there was unfinished business to attend to and like some unhappy ghost, every corner of the place would call me back until it was resolved. In my ending lies my beginning.

I sighed and pushed the button of the great milling machine and heard it whirr into activity.

18 · *An Unexpected Homecoming*

It was Spring again and I had slept long into the morning. Night shift at the Magna Products had drained me, and sleeping during the day was a routine I never quite got used to. The incessant chattering of the birds outside my window and the warm May sun now filling the room disturbed me so that I stretched lazily and lay there wide awake. From my bed in the tiny front room of the cottage, I could see trees in blossom all the way up the valley. From time to time, I heard Patty pulling the wooden truck that Harry had made for her, scraping past the window, as she followed Gwen about the garden. Gwen would talk to her in a caring baby manner, the pair of them keeping up an amusing conversation. Patty was a quick, intelligent child. I never ceased to be amazed and delighted at her serious little face when she was trying to work things out for herself. All my free weekends were spent with my daughter. Ever since her birth there had been a special bond between us that I swore would never be broken like the one between my mother and me. From the very moment of conception, I had spoken to her, convinced totally that she would be a girl. The dream of a cottage by the sea, had been for the two of us only. Sometimes the dream, in which John did not figure, would fill me with guilt, but it remained just the same.

I yawned and then proceeded to dress. Life was peaceful here in the valley, and the past eighteen months had passed happily and quickly. I wrote often to John telling him about his daughter and the little things she did and said in the process of her growing up. His boyishly scrawled letters arrived about once a month. He spoke

89

about the boredom of life on The Rock, and sent me snaps of himself in shorts, sitting in the sun. I came out into the kitchen just as Gwen was brewing the tea.

'You smelt the tea pot,' she said, laughing.

I sat by the window, watching Patty still busily pulling the trolley along, her face red with the exertion of piling stones into it and trying to extricate the wheel from where it had lodged itself round the canvas chair leg.

'God bless her,' Gwen said, 'she ain't a ha'pporth of trouble,' and went out immediately to help Patty with the truck.

I followed Gwen into the yard, still sipping my tea, and sat in the canvas chair. Harry, who had been digging in the garden, was shouting something to Gwen and pointing excitedly up the valley. I saw Gwen shading her eyes against the sun and looking in the direction to where Harry was still pointing. Suddenly, she exclaimed,

'My God! It's our Bert.'

Then, scooping Patty up in her arms, she too pointed to a figure striding down the valley.

'It's your Daddy, my love — it's your Daddy coming home to see you.'

Dazed now, I got up and went to stand by her side. In that moment, everything seemed to be the same, yet there was a subtle difference. As I watched the tall Serviceman come nearer, I felt a slight irritation. He should have written to tell me of his homecoming. Now I knew that changes were on the way, and the house and the valley would no longer be my resting place. Then he was standing there in front of us. He discarded his kitbag and it landed with a thump on the stony ground. His eyes in that boyish, bronzed smiling face seemed more startlingly blue than ever. The lock of wayward hair over the brow was bleached a corn yellow. I went forward to greet him and stood in the circle of his arms whilst Gwen and Harry clucked excitedly around him, and Patty hid behind Gwen's skirt, not very certain yet that this stranger had anything to do with her. Finally we all moved towards the house with everybody trying to talk at once, until Gwen in her practical way marched in front saying she would put the kettle on.

It was about an hour later, when John had washed and changed, that he motioned for me to come outside, and we began to walk up the valley and towards St Anne's Woods.

'You've changed,' he said at last, after we had walked along in silence for a while. 'I can't say how, but you have changed.'

'You mean, two years and a baby later,' I replied.

He didn't answer right away, but I knew he also remembered the house at Mill Lane when he was packing to go to Gibraltar, and his last goodbye to me before Pat was born.

'Don't make it hard for me,' he said, 'you know that when a posting comes through, and I'm on active service, I have to go.' I didn't answer. In my role of Wife and Mother, it would always be me that understood and cared enough to make things easy for him. I would always have to be ready to throw him a rope when he fell into his well of loneliness. But I'd have to rely on my own strength to get myself out of its slimy depths. I suddenly remembered the night when the launch had skimmed over the mine, and the crew had all come too near that flame of reality.

'You are the only real thing,' John had said to me that night as he shivered and trembled in our lumpy bed.

Now he pulled me towards him.

'I'm home on leave for a whole fortnight — let's make the most of it.' And he bent to kiss me. It was then that I remembered I was due to go to work on the night shift that very night.

I could tell by the way that Gwen gave a genteel little sniff when I returned to the house that she was not at all in favour of the idea.

'Go to work,' she said, 'when our Bert has come all the way from Gib to spend his leave with you?' and her voice held a note of incredulity. Harry winked at John and said,

'No celebration for you tonight, my son. She doesn't have a headache, but she does have to go to work.'

I hated this exchange of male intimacy, and shot him a hostile look.

'The war effort can't stop just because servicemen come home on leave,' I retorted, and felt I had scored a point. But the sheer weight of opinion was against me, and I phoned the works to say I would not be in that night.

It became obvious that John would not be able to stay with me at the cottage, so we arranged to go to his mother's at Repton Road. Patty was used to waving me goodbye when I went to work, and was quite happy to give us a send-off from the safety of Uncle Harry's arms. I knew she would be well looked after for the week I was away. She waved to us all the way up the valley until we turned the corner and were out of sight.

My mother-in-law greeted us with warm enthusiasm, overjoyed to see her 'Darling Bertie' home safe and sound once more and to know that she would have the pleasure of his company for a whole week. She pressed her overlarge hands together and thanked the good Lord for returning 'the dear boy' back to the bosom of his family.

Later, when we were drinking tea from the best china tea service that had been hastily taken from the sideboard, she suddenly remembered that she must make up the big double bed in the front bedroom. As she passed me on her way up the stairs, she nudged my arm and whispered,

'My Bertie was conceived in that double bed.'

I slopped some tea into my saucer for she had made me jump, not from the news but from the sudden jogging of my arm.

When she returned from making the bed, she had on her outdoor things.

'Come and have a drink on me, kiddos,' she said, looking at us both. 'A nice glass of stout makes me sleep and this calls for a celebration.'

Outside, she linked her arm through John's and put him in the middle.

'Now we can both share him,' was her comment.

She walked very tall and straight and seemed proud to be on the arm of her uniformed son.

The lounge at the local was quiet and held an air of respectable decorum. Not at all like the noisy bars at Grimsby, with the crowd of servicemen and the beer-swilled table tops. Somehow, although I could not have explained why, I missed the free and easy atmosphere. Not even from the public bar was there any sound of a piano, or anyone singing — perhaps that would come later. Several of the older men came over to John to speak to him, and it was evident that they knew him well. I guessed they were fathers of school friends and caught snatches of conversation that confirmed this to be so. I sat at a corner table and watched his animated interchange of gossip for a long time. Several women came up to speak to Minnie, their gaze going swiftly to the bar when she indicated that her son stood there. He in turn would give a smile and a wave when he recognised them. For the better part of the night, the men propped up the bar and made no attempt to join us in conversation. We could have been a different breed for all the notice they took of us. In the corner, with a glass of shandy more lemonade than beer, I was bored. The drink did nothing for me except to blow me up with gas and chill my stomach. I yearned for one of those delicious egg flips, but it did not occur to me to go to the bar and ask for one or to ask Minnie to get me one. I began to yawn.

Minnie was on her second stout when I was startled to hear her comment as though she had read my thoughts,

'Have a decent drinkie on me.'

I watched her go to the bar and wondered if she was clairvoyant enough to know what I would like, but she returned with a new drink for me called port and lemon. Things brightened up considerably, and as she lifted her glass to say 'Cheers, Kid,' she gave a little giggle as her nose went into the froth at the top of her third milk stout.

'Twas the old Mill by the Stream,' she began to sing, holding the glass away from her and giving a slight burp at the end of the line. I glanced around the room, but nobody was taking any notice. I had to turn away to hide the laugh. It was some time later, when the barhand was collecting empty glasses and putting them on a tray, that Minnie decided to burst into song. The barhand had reached our table and was scooping up her empty glass when she reached out to grab his arm and began to serenade him. Whilst he gave an embarrassed little laugh and tried discreetly to disengage his arm, she gave a rendering that would have done Florrie Ford full justice. When she came to the end of the song, in a fit of sheer devilry and making my voice as common as possible, I joined in the last line.

'You are my heart's delight, I love you Nellie Dean. Oh sweet Nellie Dean.'

The barman grinned, and continued wiping down the tables. A voice called 'Time, gentlemen, please!'

I giggled and said to Minnie, 'They don't mean us, so we can stay and have another drink.'

John got hastily down from the bar stool and hurried over to help Minnie into her coat and usher us both through the door.

When we got back to the house, Minnie was begging me not to make her laugh anymore or she would wet her knickers. We both sat on the bottom step and laughed hysterically. Without a word, John brushed past us and went up to bed. Beer always made John sleep. When finally I followed him up, he was already snoring under the eiderdown.

'At least I shall be safe tonight,' I thought, and giggled again.

By the end of the week, he was showing signs of

boredom. The sea called him, and he said he missed the companionship and the team spirit of the lads. He was also out of fags. To run out of 'the weed' was a dire calamity, second to none. When he came down to breakfast and discovered the empty packet, his face wore a dark look like rain clouds about to descend. I pushed a cup of tea in front of him and waited for the outburst.

'How can I drink tea, woman, without a fag?'

His mother came into the room at that precise moment, wearing a faded dressing gown and shuffling along in a pair of slippers several sizes too big.

'Dear boy,' she cooed, 'out of ciggies?'

She immediately went to the dresser where three jugs of varying sizes dangled from brass hooks along the shelf. From the middle jug, she extracted a fresh pack of fags and beamed with pleasure when her beloved Bertie threw his arms about her neck and kissed her. The black cloud vanished and the sun came out. When his gaze travelled over to me sitting there watching this little domestic scene, it seemed that the look conveyed a clear message.

'This is the sort of thing my mother does for me, and because I like it I want you to do the same.'

Learning by example, I thought and remembered how Aunt Ada used to walk through to the kitchen after my mother had made a cherry cake and had commenced hacking away at it.

'Our Denny do like your homemade cake,' she used to say, still cutting away. Sitting on the arm of the chair, I would mimic her,

'A piece for today, and a piece for tomorrow.'

Why did mothers and aunties spoil the lads so?

I think John was as relieved as I was when a few days later a temporary posting to Ilfracombe came through, and I saw him off at Temple Meads station. I always seemed to be waving goodbye, and John seemed always a shadowy figure just popping up from time to time, not staying long enough for either of us to get to know the other. Another spell of overseas service was due, so the period at Ilfracombe would be a short one. Impulsively, he leaned out of the carriage window and said, as though the thought had only just struck him,

'If I can get digs, perhaps you and the nipper could spend a few days down there. I'll write and let you know.'

I couldn't wait to get back to the cottage. The surface of the pond was ruffled by this sudden arrival of my husband and somehow I had a premonition that the next phase of my life would not be so peaceful.

True to this hunch, and all too soon, I received a letter from John saying that he had found digs if I still fancied a holiday. He went on to explain that they had not been easy to find, because the damn Yanks were everywhere, chucking their brass around like confetti, waggling nylons in front of the girls, together with boxes of chocolate that made the girls fall for them hook, line and sinker.

Overpaid, oversexed and over here was how he described them. The weather was perfect, so I let my heart rule my head. I threw some things for me and Pat in a suitcase and made ready to leave. I was also ever so slightly inquisitive to see all those damned Yanks.

19 · *Those Damned Yanks*

It was true that the damn Yanks were everywhere. After John had met us and escorted us into the main street at Ilfracombe, a jeep full of uniformed airmen shrieked to a halt in front of a hotel. They all tumbled out, noisy and brash. My guess was that this peaceful little seaside resort had never seen anything quite like it before. John watched them with disgust. Still piloting me by the arm, he hurried us past the hotel and on towards the top end of the street. Outside a cafe there were more Yanks, sitting at little round tables with bright coloured wide umbrellas, sipping cool drinks from a straw. As we passed them, one endeavoured to engage me in conversation.

'Say lady, we sure like this piece of little ol' England,' he drawled, and I looked up to see a very tanned and good looking American smiling at me.

'If you so much as encourage one of those Yanks,' John was hissing in my ear.

'I will contrive to resist a mad and wild impulse to hurl myself at the first Yank I meet,' I hissed back at him, and wondered why he had ever bothered to bring me here if the damn Yanks bothered him all that much. It seemed to me that, as a married man, it shouldn't bother him at all if they took every female there. I decided I would not push my luck by asking him about that, but followed as he strode very fast along the road.

The guest house that he brought me to had an attic. I might have known it would be ours. To get up to this tiny room, you pulled down a ladder. Patty thought it was a wonderful game. I did not. I saw the disadvantages of manoeuvring the thing at urgent times, like in the middle of the night and early morning in order to get to the toilet, which was on the landing on the next floor down. I hoped the bed was not near a wall. It would be just my luck to have to crawl over the both of them when duty called.

I breathed a sigh of relief when I saw the bed set squarely in the middle of the room with only just enough room to walk around it. There was actually one more piece of furniture in the room, and that was a chest of drawers. A rough piece of wood with hooks attached to it served as a place to hang clothes, and around the room was an assortment of tapestry texts. One proclaimed 'Behold, I stand at the door and knock'. 'Feed my lambs' begged another. Over the head of the bed was a king sized masterpiece, 'I am the unseen guest in every household', which I thought was a bit intimidating.

'Well,' I said to John, 'if only I had packed my chastity belt, between you and the good Lord, I would be well protected.'

I tested the bed by lying full length on it and bouncing up and down. I distrusted all beds after the lumpy sack back at Grimsby. To my delight, I found myself on a feather mattress. This was a bonus indeed.

When we prepared for bed later that night, I deliberately put Patty in the middle of us and ignored the pained expression on John's face. I told him that he had omitted to feed his flock or answer the door, and we could not make love because the unseen guest might be having an eyeful from the top of the bedpost. He gave an angry twist round to the wall away from me, taking all the bedclothes with him. It was not such a loss on a hot July night and in a feather bed that one could sink into. I was asleep in no time flat.

I was awakened by the sound of a woman's voice singing the latest hit song whilst brushing down the stairs.

> *You must remember this,*
> *A kiss is just a kiss,*
> *A sigh is just a sigh.*
> *The fundamental things apply*
> *As time goes by.*

I lay for a long time listening to her sweet voice until she must have completed the stairs, and I heard the low tones of another person talking to her. No doubt she was being given other work to do.

I yawned, and began to dress to go in search of breakfast. When at first I did not see John anywhere, I surmised that he had gone to the base. I was surprised therefore to see him on the landing ready to help Patty down. Over breakfast, he offered to show us around Ilfracombe. He had a day off and we might as well make the most of it. The following Saturday would be my 26th birthday and our fourth wedding anniversary.

It took me by surprise, then, when he stopped at a gem stone shop to ask if there was anything in the window that took my fancy, and when I began to show interest in a tray of silver rings, he invited me into the shop and asked the assistant to show me some. I was particularly interested in a small black onyx ring that fitted the little finger of my right hand and cost a fiver. It felt and looked just right, and I was delighted when John passed the money over the counter to pay for it.

To get to the beach, we had to go through a quaint little tunnel. Patty was not impressed with the rather boisterous waves that broke onto the shore with the incoming tide. When the waves receded, they took with them tons of pebbles and sand, and made a great sucking swishing sound. Those same waves pounded the formation of rocks along the shoreline and sent spray high in the air. Only when the tide was on the ebb and left behind safe little rock pools and warm inlets would it be safe to take her to that part of the beach to play.

We came away from the beach and made our way to a green velvet stretch of land called Hillsborough. We had bought Pat a small pink celluloid windmill on a stick. When you held it high above your head, the wind would send the tiny propellers flapping furiously around with a mad whirring clacking sound. She ran on ahead of us, laughing as she went.

At the top of the knoll, we could look right over onto another part of the beach which, from where we were standing, looked like a series of tiny coves and inlets all along the coastline. The strong sun made the sand a deep golden colour, and with the brilliant blue sky this perfect setting was enticing. From where we stood looking down, it seemed possible that one small jump would bring us onto the inviting shoreline. I allowed my gaze to wander away, up to the line of scrub at the top of the beach. Rolls of barbed wire reached all along the cliff top sticking out like a sore thumb and a stark reminder, like some obscene intrusion, that here in wartime nothing was as it seemed.

I shuddered slightly, and turned away, walking back down the hill again. I was getting hungry and John had promised us a fish and chip tea. He knew a cafe that sold a smashing plate of fish and chips.

Joe's Cafe was also in the High Street. You couldn't miss it, as it had his name in big black letters painted over the door. Joe did everything himself, there was no assistant. Ilfracombe slumbered in an easy-going pace that seemed never to have altered. The arrival of the Yanks brought only a tolerant acceptance of their high spirits. The war would not last long and the Yanks would go home. Joe kept the fish already filleted, in a bucket under the sink. When he was ready, he would take the fish from the bucket and flop it around in the batter before popping it into the sizzling hot fat. Joe was talkative and informative. With his sleeves rolled up, and a white apron round his waist, he told us that the small hotel over the road was his, and that before the war he and his wife could depend only on the summer visitors that came there. That was why he had opened up the cafe as another source of income for the winter. All this had changed with the arrival of the Yanks who had commandeered both the hotels in the main street. His wife ran the place now. He helped her all he could during the day, but enjoyed the work in the cafe and opened it up for the Yanks now at tea time. His wife was looking for a bit of help serving the breakfast and helping with the beds.

'Just the job for you,' he said looking at me, 'that's if you are interested.'

Walking back to the guest house, I mentioned to John that I would think about that offer. I began to enthuse about the nursery that Joe said was just around the corner, but stopped suddenly when I saw the anger on his face.

'I want you to promise me that you will go home when my posting comes through. Promise me now,' he said, and turned in the road to take hold of my shoulders, not roughly but to stress the point.

'I'm damned if I will,' I replied, facing him and twice as angry. 'What's so wrong with wanting to take a job in a hotel? It beats a dusty stinking machine shop any day.'

The thought crossed my mind that there were no Yanks at the Magna Products, only middle aged men who were exempt from the war.

'If it's the damn Yanks that you are afraid of, I have just as much suspicion about you with all the damn girls in uniform.'

We walked back to the guest house in silence, both of us angry now. Without a word, he turned on his heel and left us. It might be several days before he had another precious day off. I looked down at the tiny ring on the little finger of my right hand. Wearing a ring on that finger was a sign of independence. My independence and John's stubborn streak always seemed to meet head on. Somehow, I could not find a way to defuse the situation and he could find no way to cope with a strong independent woman. In the right way, I could be guided, yes. But I was damned if I would be controlled and manipulated. I resolved that I would go to see Joe's wife to find out what the job was all about. That could do no harm. The more I thought about working in a hotel, the more possible it became. Before drifting off to sleep, I felt sad that the day had started off so well and ended so badly. John's birth sign was Cancer the Crab, a water sign, and mine was Leo the Lion, a fire sign. I concluded angrily that his water was always putting out my fire.

The very fact that I did not see John the following day, which left us with a long boring day to fill, did nothing to lessen my determination to go round to the hotel to enquire about the job. In fact, the moment I stepped outside the guest house after breakfast, my feet seemed to guide me there. Joe's wife was plump and pleasant. She was also quick and efficient, and very well dressed.

She was smiling at us now with her eyebrows slightly raised as I explained that her husband had mentioned something about her needing some help. As if I had said a magic word, she opened the glass door wide and invited us inside. She led the way through into a large bright kitchen and beckoned to us to sit down at a big wooden table. She asked Pat if she would like a glass of orange and then proceeded to pour out two cups of tea from a large tea pot. I said I did not know her name.

'I'm Doreen Cummins,' she said. 'You can call me Dora. Everybody else does.'

She put a piece of cake in front of Pat then leaned forward briskly.

'While she's wading through that little lot, you and I can get down to business. Now, I need some help with the breakfast in the morning, and of course, there will be the washing up and the dining hall to be tidied. Beds to be made and laundry to be checked every Friday.' She paused to look at Pat. 'There is a nursery round the corner for your daughter. She will have children to play with. That will be good for her, don't you think?' She didn't wait for me to answer but went straight on. 'You could be away by one o'clock every day and I would give you two pounds a week, plus your breakfast and bed as well if you've nowhere to stay. How does that suit you?'

I blinked. Gosh! The money was a king's ransom with the breakfast and a bedroom on top. I thought of the pathetic twelve shillings allowance which was my service pay. Now I was going to get treble that for just a part-time job. A nod was all that was needed to clinch the deal. And I could start on Monday if that was alright with me. All was right with my world at that moment. It was only when Dora had seen us to the door and, still smiling, waved goodbye to us, that I suddenly remembered John. What if he refused to let me go?

'Rubbish,' I thought, 'he couldn't, he wouldn't. Would he?'

My heart gave a great thud when, as we reached the cafe, I saw a familiar figure seated outside drinking coffee. All trace of his anger had vanished, and when he saw us, he got up quickly to help us into a chair and to order a drink for us. It was after the drink was finished and we were walking back to the digs, that I blurted out rather clumsily,

'Look, John, I have taken the job.'

It was out now, and I screwed up my eyes and waited for the bang. When nothing happened, I grew brave enough to open my eyes to look at him. To my surprise he never said a word. Presently he said ever so quietly,

'I guessed you would.'

I rushed on regardless. I had to tell him about the bedroom which was twin bedded and had a toilet and bathroom adjoining. Dora had said that he could stay as well — any time; whenever, in fact, he had a day off or a weekend. I was sure he would love Dora. I stole a sideways glance. He wasn't mad, I could see that. Quite amiable. When finally he did break the silence, it was to tell me that the following weekend he would be off and as it was my birthday he would come to the hotel and stay. Saturday he had a surprise in store for me so he wanted me to be ready to make as early a start as possible. Then he kissed me and was gone. I blinked. Well, that was a turn up for the book. Capitulation without a struggle.

I paid the bill at the guest house and moved into the hotel on Sunday, ready to take up my duties the following morning, early. Joe took Patty to the nursery and came back to report that she had been as good as gold. I buttered piles of rolls and toast, put them on plates and sent them along a smooth white counter top, along with mountains of sausages and beans. Bacon and eggs was served three times a week and always on Sundays. I sloshed coffee into rows of mugs set over a wire tray to take the spillage, and tackled the piles and piles of dirty crocks, never stopping until the last one had been dried and put away. Dora and I then sat for half an hour over a well earned cuppa before going upstairs to tackle the beds. On Fridays, the dirty washing was sent down a shute to be collected in bins and sent to the laundry. On Tuesdays, the clean bedding was checked and put away in the cupboard. The work was hard but rewarding and Dora was full of energy. We got on well together and she was a firm favourite with the Yanks.

As promised, John arrived at the hotel on Friday night, and was introduced to Dora and Joe. Joe and John were soon talking about the High Speed Launches of the RAF, and Dora thought my husband was 'a grand fella'. She shooed me off at twelve-thirty the following day, when she realised it was my birthday and John wanted to take me out.

20 · *Keep Out — Things are Not What They Seem*

A blazing sun beating down on a white main street made a shimmering heat haze which dazzled and hurt our eyes and drained us of all energy as we walked along. I was glad when we turned towards Hillsborough and the belt of grass that was more restful to our eyes. The faint smell of driftwood mingled with seaweed and dross from the shoreline as we reached the top of the knoll. As we stood there with a soft breeze blowing about us, the tiny cove below seemed more inviting than ever. It was only when I became aware that, as we walked, we were dropping down towards one of those white dotted coves that I began to look anxiously at John. We were actually walking along by the barbed wire fencing. A huge board with bold red letters warned us that this was Government Property, Private, Keep Out.

'Do you really mean to ignore all this?' I said, stopping to look at the warning notice.

John had Patty perched high on his shoulders. The silence all around us was broken only by the slight breeze that made the folded sails on the windmill that Pat was still carrying rotate furiously. He didn't answer, but had gone on striding ahead. I followed feeling slightly apprehensive. He stopped a bit further on and when I came up to him I could see where an opening had been deliberately cut in the barbed wire fence and rolled back to make a space just wide enough to squeeze through. John and Patty were first through the opening. I still hesitated.

'Come on,' John was calling. 'The lads found this way in, make the most of it while you can.'

Throwing all caution to the wind, I raced after the both of them down to the water's edge. Patty caught some of our excitement and began to jump up and down. We took off all our clothes except for our panties and waded into the water until it reached our waists. It was a safe beach, flat and firm to our feet. I was glad that it did not shelve deeply. We lifted Patty up over the gentle waves as they rolled in, leaving a band of white frothy foam on the edge of the sand. John took a header into the sea and began to swim — a clumsy breast-stroke so that he floundered about awkwardly and spat and spluttered like some small whale. I began to laugh and after a few seconds he came panting up to us again and admitted he was out of practice.

We ran in and out of the water like small children and lay on the hot sand with the sun drying us. John took my hand and we waded out to where the water covered my shoulders. I could not swim, but he held my hands with those beautiful hands of his and encouraged me to bob up and down to get used to the water and not be afraid of it. It was a perfect day, with the continental blue of the sky and the hot sun.

We had been asleep for some time when I felt John stir and when I opened my eyes, he was dressing quickly. My first thought was that he must get back to the base, then I remembered that it was only Saturday and he had the whole weekend. He didn't say anything, but I thought I detected a sense of urgency in this unexpected move. I called to Pat who came obediently but looked at me with a puzzled frown that her play was to be curtailed. We walked back up the beach to where the rolled barbed wire

105

with that defiant cut in it became our exit now. Passing the big notice with the bold red letters, making the word DANGER stand out, my gaze caught and held on the word. Just for a second in my imagination, I saw the red letter blur over and run down the board. The paint seemed to hang from the bottom of the letters and looked like red, red blood.

I glanced back at the cove. It still held that innocent serenity, the golden sand fringed with white froth and banded around like a framed picture from the azure blue of the sky. Why was it then, that as I scanned the board everything was alright again, but still there was a wrong note like a twang from the lower end of the scale? It had something to do with the board.

The war department would not fence off that stretch of beach for nothing. I felt myself hold my breath. We had been foolish to take such a risk, but I could not dare to voice the dreadful thought that was in my mind, that the beach was probably mined. John did not release the hold he had on Patty. In fact, he did not put her down to walk, until the path had been skirted, and we were once more on top of the knoll and the velvet green of the grass was there in front of us.

All through August, the heat wave continued. There were times when the torrid atmosphere of the kitchen sapped my energy and my spirits flagged. With every window open, and not a breath of air to encourage the slightest flap, Ilfracombe slumbered lazily in the summer heat and seemed to brood silently. Even the damn Yanks, usually energetic and noisy, sat around, their long legs sprawled out in front of them whilst they lounged in the chairs. An unnatural calm pervaded everywhere.

I had been at the hotel for five weeks and was beginning to settle in. John came often and stayed. I still could not fathom out why he had accepted the situation so calmly, but concluded that I would leave well alone. He was liked and accepted at the hotel by Dora and Joe. Much more to my surprise, he even stopped to talk to the

106

damn Yanks. That made me scratch my head in wonder, but I did not comment.

All through September and well into October, the beautiful weather continued. The trees retained their autumnal glory and no cold wind blew off their leaves. Only one thing marred the natural orderliness of my life. For some weeks I had been feeling listless and irritable. I watched the Yanks at breakfast time consuming mountains of food and swilling it down with great gulps of coffee. I watched with actual disgust their distasteful habit of eating and drinking at the same time.

'It's enough to make one vomit.'

I brushed aside the thrill of fear my words brought up. No, that couldn't be true. I had been working through all the heat and that was the reason I felt this way.

A week later, it was confirmed when suddenly in the middle of sliding a tray of bacon along the counter, a sudden dash to the toilet resulted in my being sick. I leaned by the sink splashing my face with cold water. No mistaking that sign.

'Oh no,' I wailed, 'oh no.'

John's posting had finally come through, and he was off to Ceylon. On Saturday I was going to have a farewell drink with him at the local pub. The awful irony of life. I was going to Ceylon before the damned war had hit that one on the head. Now he would be going there whilst I . . . I began to cry. I wouldn't even be able to stay here and work. The dream of the cottage was fading, along with the desperate knowledge that Gwen would not be able to house me and another baby.

Miserably I sat opposite John in the pub on that Saturday night. He leaned over to ask,

'Are you alright, Pet, you're very quiet?'

'No, I am not alright. I am pregnant. On the eve of your disappearing yet once more into the sunset, I am about to be grounded.'

He sat there quietly finishing his beer. Then, getting up with the same deliberate movements, he walked slowly

107

John with Joyce and Pat on his only leave in 1941

to the bar to order another. I could have screamed. He sat for a long time just looking at me, his expression conveying nothing.

'You will go home now.' The words spoken so quietly, came like a blow. There was no commiseration in their tone, not even a question. Just a cold contrived demand with which he knew I would have to comply.

'You will go home now.'

'Damn you,' I said almost inaudibly, 'damn you.'

There was no fire in that sad little response. I was defeated.

21 · *Education is the Thing*

'Vee,' I wailed, some three months later, 'just what am I going to do?'

'We had the Yanks here.' Vee was switching the subject and I looked sharply at her as she went on. 'Ces would have put a bolt on the front door to stop me from even going to speak to them. They came all along this street asking for digs. Most men probably felt the same way.'

'And how does it feel not to be trusted?' My voice rose in anger.

'I wouldn't have gone against Ces like you went against John,' Vee said, 'I would have been too scared.'

'What are you saying, Vee?' and I emphasised the last word vehemently. 'Are you telling me that the baby is a kind of reprisal for going against him? Am I being forced to believe that he is capable of such trickery? I am beginning to feel more like a Queen Bee everyday,' I went on, 'my only role is to reproduce, to lie there for his enjoyment and for the benefit of the next generation. He's not even there when it's all happening.'

'I've got three kids,' Vee cut in, 'and my ol' man is not even around now to see them grow up.'

I suddenly saw my mother and understood how she must have felt when, after her marriage to Dad and the birth of her son six months later, she had found herself pregnant with me. How well I remembered her words.

'You cannot make a woman love her child just by virtue of the fact that a man can make her pregnant.'

'God help me,' I cried out in despair, 'I almost hate

109

him. And feel that I am creating the same set of circumstances that my mother was in. What can I do?'

'Come and have a cuppa,' Vee coaxed. She escaped into the kitchen and left me with dark thoughts I could not voice. She came back a few minutes later with two mugs of steaming hot tea and a couple of home made cakes on a tray. Again I poured out my tale of woe. Poor old Vee. I leaned on her very heavily that day.

'All that lovely money I saved was supposed to go on a house, instead it now has to buy a layette and a bloody pram. I ant determined, Vee, I won't yank this one around in a wheelbarrow.'

I sniffed and felt a rush of self pity for the shattered dream, the loss of my dream house. Another surge of anger welled up inside of me. There was one thing that I would make damned sure wouldn't happen to my children that happened to me — one thing that my mother had not done for me that I would do for my children.

'Yes,' I vowed to Vee, as I sat there sipping my tea, even if it meant that I had to take a job scrubbing floors, I would make sure my kids had an education. None of this leaving school at fourteen with no skill or learning behind you. With an education plus a skill, they would have a choice, with no choice there was no freedom. I had seen the look of utter futility so many times in women's eyes. Maybe in some small way I could try to change things for them.

I remembered how I felt on that day I left school at fourteen. How angry and inadequate. I wanted more learning, not to be thrust into an unskilled job scrubbing coal cellars or packing corsets. When I left Vee, I was ready to fight.

'I'll do it even if it kills me,' I said.

I settled back into the life and the identity of Repton Road with Minnie. The house was one of a terrace, all the same, with no back entrance. The door opened into a passage through to the back door. There was a parlour in the front, a middle room with french doors onto the back yard occupied by Emmy, and a kitchen with an open fire in the corner. Opening the door always made us choke in the billowing smoke. Finally, there was a dingy little stone floored scullery with a mangle on the far back wall and a marble topped table. A giant iron stove with a black band round the middle took up most of the space. It took ten men to carry that stove away. The privy was outside, along with a small shed. Upstairs were three bedrooms — Gertie in the back, Ma in the middle and John and I in the big front room with a double bed and a table. The house was very dark and cold.

Like so many other similar roads, the kids played there and it was their playground. When it was time for Patty to come in for tea or bedtime, I pushed up the window to call her from the bedroom. On sunny days in Summer, the Granddads would sit outside the front door and keep an eye on the children, shouting to them to get out of the road when a car or motor bike came by. With fathers away fighting, the 'oldies' played an important role, chastising the kids in a form of discipline that they respected. Sat in his chair by the front door, grandad could chat to passers-by, and he had a sense of being wanted and of belonging.

Monday was ash bin day, and because this row of terraced houses had no back entrance, the bins had to be dragged through the passageway and set down outside the gate. Most rubbish receptacles were in a sorry state, with sides bashed in and bottoms that threatened to disgorge contents at any moment. The Corporation dustmen displayed a healthy contempt for the owner's bins; they had long mastered the art of heaving them up on to their shoulders, disposing of the waste in one well timed tip up, with the same expert elbow action sending the bins skidding in the direction of its house like beer mugs sent spinning along a beer soaked table top. The bin lids fared even worse. They were sent spinning through the air rather like a game of Hoop-La with about as much success at hitting the target as the contestants in the fair ground. When the last bin had been emptied and the dust cart had disappeared round the corner, there were mopping up operations to be done. The smelly bin was retrieved and carted back to the garden. The passageway was swept, and several buckets of water were thrown down on the path just outside the gate and it was brushed clean. Finally, the window ledges got a wipe and the brass step was polished. Monday was a real old gossip day. With so many women wielding a brush or going great guns with a polishing duster, they could pass the time of day to the neighbour over the way, or with the metal polish tins still in their hands, they would linger in little knots to discuss any recent happening in the street. Net curtains twitched as their owners peeped to see who was talking to who, and the whole street became like an Indian settlement, with gossip like smoke signals drifting in all directions.

On Friday, the whole process was repeated after the coalman had called. He humped the bags of coal on his back through the hall and kitchen out into the scullery to a coal hole that was situated in the far corner, usually right by the side of the huge mangle that graced that side of the wall. Because of the position of the handle on this giant contraption, the poor man had to be extremely careful when he twisted round to drop the coal. Several very colourful expletives accompanied the three bags of coal he dropped into our coal hole, and for which we handed over two shillings each.

After I had taken my turn at sweeping the hall and

giving the brass step a rub up for the weekend, I carted the coal scuttle all the way upstairs, for the fire that I lit even night. Fortunately, the chimney never had to be swept whilst I was there, and although when the wind was high the smoke blew down the chimney, I would not like to dwell on what it might have been like if the chimney had needed sweeping.

My mother-in-law had found it necessary to let a couple of her rooms. As she explained,

'It's just to keep body and soul together.'

Her second husband, Fred, John's father, had died in 1942, the year after Pat was born. John was overseas when the news reached him. Fred had never been a robust man, and after their marriage had stayed around long enough to produce a son and then had gone home to his mother. None of his family had approved of Minnie pursuing Fred because of the many years difference in their ages, and by way of defending herself she would defiantly exclaim,

'Well, we clicked and that was all there was to that.' Now Minnie was slightly impoverished because there had been few worldly goods to pass on to his widow. 'I loved him,' Minnie said simply, and took a pinch of snuff.

The two tenants she took in were as different as chalk is from cheese, and they hated each other. Emmy was a meek and mild little soul and scuttled into her room as soon as she heard Gert's brash and common voice. She had the added advantage of being able to lock her middle room door and disappear into the scullery and the yard through the french doors, and she buried herself in her room like some small dormouse, only emerging to pay the tradesmen or to swoop on her evening paper as it slid through the door, before Gertie, who was now in the best parlour and could see the paper man coming through the gate, got there first to have a sly look through. It was a nightly ritual, with both of them ready and waiting at the slightly open door, both ready to outwit the other.

Gertie was as rough as Emmy said she was, and worked

at Thrissels, the Rope Factory at Brislington. The stories that she told about the daily doings at the factory were extremely lurid. At the end of each tale she would laugh in such a way that it sounded like hitting a high note and prolonging it. Emmy said she was 'as common as muck and just as stupid'. Surprisingly enough, she was also good natured, and Minnie, whom Gertie called 'Ma', got on very well with her. On Fridays, they went to the pub together, Minnie walking stiff and straight, nodding like royalty to all who passed her, and Gertie with her loud voice and almost imbecilic laugh, by her side.

'Taking Ma for a drop of how's yer Father,' she informed acquaintances who passed them. 'Ma likes her glass of stout — right Ma?'

When Gertie came home from work and passed through the kitchen on her way to the scullery, she would always engage Minnie in conversation while she was waiting for her tea to cook on the stove and for some time now, the pair of them had been following the exploits of a young couple that had recently moved into a house further down the road. The young wife usually left for work about the same time that Gertie did and sometimes walked part of the way with her. The plot began to thicken, especially when Mrs Turnball over the road noticed from behind the leaves of the aspidistra that ten minutes after the wife had closed the front door, a brazen slip of a girl wearing a putty coloured coat and red boots had knocked at this same house and had been admitted by 'that lazy git of a husband of hers'. Gertie had a habit of telling her stories twice. 'Did you hear what I said, Ma? One goes out — t'other comes in.'

The laugh rose to a hysterical pitch and at this point, the laugh and not the joke always made me double up with mirth. We all wondered exactly when Mrs Turnball would decide to tell the woman, and what would happen after that.

Towards the end of May, we had an air raid. I was in bed and muttering curses because I did not want to push

114

the large lump under my pinny down the stairs, and sit, uncomfortable, in the cupboard. Gertie's voice rose to a shriek as the sirens wailed and the first two bombs fell rather too close for comfort. Ma called out that she couldn't find her teeth or her knickers.

'Never mind yer teeth Ma, just make sure you put yer bloomers on.'

By this time, we had all assembled under the stairs and were either crouching or sitting on the mattress that covered the floor. Eight more bombs fell on the city that night, each one close enough to make the house shake, the dull thuds making us close our eyes and hold our breath. We heard the raider turn and head for home and a long silence followed before the All Clear sounded.

We didn't know it then, but that was the last load of bombs to fall on Bristol. The end of the war was in sight. Gertie laughed when she saw Minnie with her hands clasped together, and said to me,

'If a whizz bang had come through the roof tonight, Ma would have been glad that she had her clean knickers on!'

The next day, we heard that the first two bombs had dropped at St Peter's Rise at Bedminster, just one district away. Another two had fallen at Abbots Lea. You could trace the trail of them right across the city. Fortunately, there were not many casualties, but a lot of damage was done.

However, I was now eight months pregnant and flagging in spirits. Having a baby never made me bloom and I was never in love with it. I was relieved when Gwen offered to take Patty with her down to the cottage. I howled with fatigue and at Patty's tearful face. She did not understand what it was all about. Even the promise of a baby brother or sister did not appease her and another separation was something she did not understand.

I did not buy a pram, there would have been no room for it in the tiny space behind the glass door. At least the news on the wireless was good, Montgomery had halted Rommel at El Alamein, and had pushed him back over the Libyan Desert. The Russians were chasing the Germans throughout the Eastern European countries and, although we did not know it at the time, here on the home front our troops were preparing for a landing in France. On the eve of this great event, at about 7:30 on the evening of June 5th, once again I called for the ambulance to get me to the hospital for the birth of my second child.

23 · *Frenchay Manor and Daughter Number Two*

Frenchay Manor was still standing in 1944. The Yanks had acquired several acres of this prime site to build a hospital for the troops. It was a very up-to-date hospital, the design of which England had never seen before, comprising wards leading off great long corridors.

The Manor itself was now a maternity ward, and it was to this once beautiful house that the ambulance clanged its way on that night so many years ago. I remember it so well because, when I was helped up the wide carpetless staircase, and into a brightly-lit delivery room, I was surprised to find American and English staff working together there. If I had any fears that my second delivery would be a repetition of the first, they were swept away as soon as I encountered the trio of doctor and two nurses who smilingly came forward to greet me and immediately put me at my ease. As the stages of labour progressed, I was helped and encouraged, and the utter relief that at all times there was a hand to hold and cling to was the biggest help of all. In fact, at one stage I was convinced that I was being mistaken for somebody else.

I gave birth to Jacqueline at 2:30 on the morning of

June 6th. She was a compact sixteen inch, eight and a half pound little bundle and the easiest birth of all my four babies, for I was destined to have two more after her. There was one thing I found unique and plucked up courage to query afterwards. I gave birth to this baby in a sitting position, propped against the doctor's chest, which I found easier in every way. Being able to see what was going on around you was more rewarding than gazing dejectedly at bright lights and the ceiling. However, in my particular case, the reason was a slightly complicated one, and it was explained to me that because of a retroversion (a tilted womb) it had been necessary for the doctor to gently press down on my stomach to allow the baby a safe passage into the birth canal. So the simple explanation was that this had been the best way to deal with the situation.

I called the new baby Jacqueline partly because it was my father's favourite name, partly out of a sense of gratitude for the doctor, who told me that he had a daughter whose name was Jacky. Even the doctor commented on the colour of her eyes, which were a cornflower blue just like her Dad's. When I was wheeled back to the ward, I breathed a sigh of relief that it had all been got over in so short a time and with comparative ease. I had been dreading it. I went to sleep almost immediately. The next morning we were awakened by Sister walking briskly into the ward and exclaiming excitedly,

'Isn't it wonderful, Mothers, our troops have just landed in Normandy!'

There was none of the trouble with feeding that I had experienced with Patty, and Jacky after a few preliminary snuffles found what she was looking for and guzzled away contentedly. Only one thing marred the serenity of my twelve day stay there. One baby disturbed the normal quiet of the nursery and howled for long periods, sometimes well into the night. We all speculated as to whose baby it might be, with half of us dismissing

117

the possibility that it could be ours. Then, when the day dawned bright and clear for my departure, they brought a transformed little Jacky to me and placed her in my arms. She looked so sweet and so angelic in the dainty things that I had packed for her, rather like a Gainsborough painting of Bubbles that one found on tins of biscuits and chocolate boxes. I stood gazing down at her, she was so exquisite.

'Maybe we shall get some peace at night in the nursery now,' the nurse said.

I saw my American doctor briefly before I left. He wished me well and called me by my Christian name. As I sat opposite him, I recalled that night when he had first requested that I tell him my first name. I had been so surprised to hear that soft, almost Southern, American drawl that I had almost wanted to giggle and mimic:

'Well, honey lamb, honey baby, honey chile, ma name is Joyce. Now ain't that something.'

I was glad now that I hadn't done so. Gratitude for all this man had done for me placed him high in my esteem. Like the films, or stories from books, I held the romantic notion that he was the type of male image I should have searched for and found. Mercifully, life had not as yet battered me enough to prove that heroes can have feet of clay.

The interview was professional and lasted long enough to explain about the retroversion syndrome. Apparently it was not a serious or uncommon condition. So long as my medical practioner was in possession of all the facts, in the event of a subsequent birth, the procedure that had accompanied my baby's birth could be repeated. However, and here he paused to consider his next words,

'Sometimes, not always,' he said cautiously, 'any future birth could get harder, especially as the woman gets older. The ideal family quota for you, my dear, might be what you now have, although I might add that this is a matter for you and your husband to decide and not I. Advice is all I am able to give.'

I felt embarassed, as though he were telling me that I was only half a woman. The inability to feed Patty, the smallness of my breasts, made it self evident that I would not be able to continue feeding this eight and a half pounder for long, and now one more thing to have to contend with seemed hard. I wanted so much to blurt out that two babies were more than enough for me to cope with, and what could I do to prevent another pregnancy? I felt myself blushing. I could not talk about these things, even to a doctor. Anger made me suddenly mumble something unintelligible, gather up my infant, and fly from the room.

The sky was a continental blue the morning I took my leave of Frenchay Manor. In the taxi, as it sped along the Fishponds Road and sharp left into Royate Hill to bypass the centre and skirt the two districts into Brislington once more, I had time to reflect on my reticence to discuss something that was becoming very urgent to me. I was resolved that I was going to tell John, at the very first opportunity, that two babies and no home was enough for me to be going on with. It seemed ridiculous that the subject of sex was such a delicate one that I shrank from talking about it both to John and to a doctor. It was an issue that had to be broached, but I was at a complete loss how to resolve it.

Jacky was as changeable as her birth sign, which is Gemini, the Twins. One moment she could lie contented and angelic in her cot, the next moment the lusty yell that disturbed all the babies in the nursery now disturbed not only the household, but most of the neighbours at night as well. At those times, nothing and nobody could appease her, no matter how much we tried. In the end, having made sure that she was dry and comfortable, with no pins or horrid windy bumps bothering her, I developed a hard of hearing side and let her bawl it out. Sometimes, from sheer exhaustion, I might drift off to sleep in the early hours of the morning and wake to find her, wide eyed and angelic, quietly playing with her

119

fingers. Her hands held some kind of fascination for her, and she looked at them for hours.

It came as a bit of a shock when, six weeks after the birth of Jacky, I received a letter from John to say he was back in England, and stationed at Pembroke Dock, one of his old bases. They would not be there for long as he was expecting another posting quite soon. They were entitled to some leave and in order that he might see his new daughter he thought it might be a good idea if he arranged some digs. I could travel down to Pembrokeshire and spend a precious fourteen days with him. He could take me around to show me different places and it would be a holiday to share together.

Instead of being elated, I was beset by fears and apprehension. The long separation and now my two babies made me feel that John was a stranger, someone who kept popping up and leaving behind shadowy memories. Now, sooner than I expected, I would have to demand that we talk about any future family and being very much aware of that stubborn streak of his, I knew that venture would not be easy. Besides, to visit Pembrokeshire with that ultimatum as a greeting would definitely not put me in a good light. Yet it had to be spoken about, it was important to me. That this should have been self-evident to my spouse as well was something that I childishly thought was my business to make him aware of, and to do it in such a diplomatic way as not to hurt his feelings. If his reaction was as I feared, it would all be my fault anyway. I couldn't win.

I told Minnie that her beloved Bertie was home and in Pembrokeshire and about his invitation to join him for a holiday. She was puzzled that I was not very enthusiastic about the reunion or the holiday. If I had told her the real reason, that my not wanting to go was because I was scared of coming home with another 'bun in the oven' she would merely have stated,

'That's life, kid — just tell him to get off at Crewe.'

24 · *Pembrokeshire and the Bosherton Lily Fields*

I knew I was going to love Pembrokeshire the moment I stepped from the train onto the quaint little station and saw the white painted seat with the bank of flowers behind it. There was a delightful smell like musk roses in the air, and it looked as though nothing had ever changed or was ever likely to change. When I dragged my battered old suitcase from the train, and set it down by the side of the white seat, everything looked so familiar, so homely, that I thought if I walked away and forgot it, the darn thing would still be there a week later. I sat with my two children in the warm August sunshine waiting for John and drinking in the peace and serenity of that magic place, for the past seemed to be all around me.

The train barely made any noise as it slid lazily out of the station and out of sight, and it was Pat who first saw her father and ran to meet him. I watched the pair of them as he bent to kiss her, and then she was holding his hand and skipping back towards us. When he came up to us on the seat, I noticed that he was as tanned as he had been when he returned from The Rock, and the wayward wave was just as blond, making him look so young and boyish. He asked about the journey whilst gazing intently at his second daughter. He placed her easily in the crook of one arm, and picked up my case with the other. So our little trio walked slowly out of the station and along a country lane that held the pungent smell of spruce and pine needles. We spoke very little, although in the train I had reflected a great deal about the sort of digs I was being taken to, and could hardly restrain the urge to ask. Past experiences had warned me never again to trust the judgement of my spouse where accommodation was concerned. Maybe it was the lazy heat of the day and the perfect moment that I did not want to shatter, but I thought that it wasn't possible to find such a thing as awful digs in so perfect a setting. When we came to the outskirts of the town, the first sign of habitation was row upon row of terraced houses with no front gardens. There seemed to be no front doors to the houses either, but in their place were brightly coloured striped canvas blinds that flapped ever so slightly in the warm breeze and revealed the brilliant shine of polished brass steps. A bus laboured snail-like up the hill and stopped about a dozen paces in front of us, disgorging about six passengers who looked at us curiously as we came up to them. Nobody spoke or gave a greeting. They merely turned and went their different ways, with the bus starting up again and moving away out of sight. I was just beginning to wonder how much further we would have to traverse this long road, when John stopped in front of a Methodist Chapel. The sandstone facade stood out boldly, and the blazing sun on that hot August day turned the warm sandstone into yet a richer rosy glow. On a wide, white paved courtyard leading from the front of the church was a notice board proclaiming in bold black letters the name of the Clergyman who would be conducting the service the following Sunday. There was an additional large poster pinned next to this piece of information, which stated that there would be a choir practice for the male voices the following Thursday in the school room. For all those attending, the keys could be obtained at the caretaker's house adjoining. Mr and Mrs Evans were the caretakers.

The house was demurely screened by a row of laurel bushes, and a black spiked iron gate which had to be lifted up in the middle to allow us to walk through; it squeaked rather badly in the process. John left it, pathetically hanging almost off its hinges, as we proceeded up the path to a side entrance with three steps and a porch with two imposing pillars on the top wide step. John found a bell push which he pulled in and out several times. Standing on the path and listening to that strident peal, I noticed that three tall cypress trees hid the garden. I peered through the foliage and was surprised to discover that only a very low wall separated the garden from the neat row of graves on the other side of the church yard.

The door was opened by a well built woman well into her sixties, with a black shawl round her shoulders and a very well kept hair bun at the nape of her neck. She beamed at us from the doorway, and it was evident from John's answering beam of a smile that the pair of them knew each other.

'Well now, my lovelies, if 'tis me you're wanting, here I am. Tired now you must be, coming all the way from Bristol and those dear babies so good and so quiet. Come in, come in now I'll run and put the kettle on, you'd like some tea now, I shouldn't wonder.'

She led the way through the hall and into a bright little kitchen at the far end of the house. The window gave a full view of the garden and the side of the chapel.

As we sat there drinking tea, with John and Mrs Evans talking easily to one another, it was explained to me that John was no stranger to this household and had walked out with their daughter Christina some few years earlier when he had been sent to Pembroke to do his training. It was strange sitting there listening about a friendship that had unfolded in a part of John's life that I knew nothing about. Inadvertently, my thoughts turned to Gord. There was no way I could have mentioned that relationship to anybody. Perhaps, in order to keep the memories evergreen, they must be kept airtight, and never allowed to see the light of day. John's questions relating to Christina's whereabouts were met by Mrs Evans with a guarded vagueness. She was over Haverfordwest way, happily married now with two boys. She filled John's cup with more tea and as she pushed the cup towards him she looked directly at me.

'Well, now, that's all in the past, and you with a lovely little family of your own.'

Then, as though she guessed my embarrassment, she changed the conversation abruptly.

'Tell me, my lovely, are you chapel?'

I nodded and almost choked on a biscuit to answer, 'Methodist'. Her eyes lit up with pleasure.

'There's nice, now. Three times we go on Sunday, and our Reverend Mr Eli Thomas is ever so nice. Providential it is that you be the same as us — not like some people I could mention around here. Never seen the inside of the Lord's house and that's a fact, proper heathen I calls it.'

Mrs Evans sniffed with righteous indignation, then took off the lid of the teapot and proceeded to fill it up once more. Mr Evans appeared in the doorway, and as soon as he saw John, strode towards him with his two arms outstretched to extend a welcome. John rose from the table, obviously delighted to see this man again, and they shook hands and thumped each other on the back like long lost brothers. At last, Mr Evans turned to me.

'We had this young man of yours staying with us when he was a whipper snapper,' he laughed. 'I had to keep an eye on him then, though — but I daresay you can keep him in order now, can't you?'

The older man thumped John playfully on the back again and laughed heartily at John's embarrassment. Mrs Evans brought more tea in the brown teapot and filled up the cups again.

'I daresay you can find your way around the house and show your wife the bedroom. You don't need me to show you, do you? I've no doubt you know every nook and cranny, eh?' She gave him a playful prod, then addressed me once more. 'Tomorrow is the Sabbath and there is one rule we all abide by on the Lord's day. There is to be no washing put on the line on Sunday. Six days labour and do all thy work, but on the seventh day thou shalt rest from thy labours.'

I was about to ask her how I could prevent my baby

124

from soiling nappies on a Sunday, and realised that my limited stock of napkins was now sadly reduced to just two. I looked around to see if there was some available dry space inside the house, but a quick survey failed to reveal anywhere suitable. I would investigate further tomorrow, on the Lord's day, I decided.

The following morning, we all slept late. When I came down into the kitchen, Mrs Evans was busy brushing down her husband's coat whilst he brushed the felt on his hat smooth with the back of his arm. He eased the stiffness of his white starched collar with a couple of circular neck movements, inserting his two thumbs into the space between the tie knot and his adam's apple. My bet was that both tie and collar would be ripped off in those intervening respites at dinner time and tea time. Mrs Evans adjusted her big, wide-brimmed hat and thrust a big gold hat pin through it and the bun at the back of her head. Then she put on her wrist long cotton gloves so that they stretched to her own finger length. She picked up her large handbag and placed the handles over her arm. When she reached the door, she turned to the sideboard and picked up two hymn books placed there. She handed one to her husband, then with a final wave to me, her wide-brimmed hat bobbing slightly, she disappeared through the hall and out through the front door.

I surveyed the bucket full of napkins under the sink and began to tackle them. I tut-tutted with annoyance about not being allowed to dry them on the line, because in the summer breeze they would have been dry in an hour. As I was squeezing and wringing them, I wondered how would she know if the damn things were on the line or not? I could have them dry and get them in long before she came home for lunch. Singing a little song, 'Hang the washing on the line Mother, oh hang the washing on the line', I picked up the bowl with the washed terry squares in and nipped quickly down the yard. From the open window of the chapel came the strains of 'The Church's one foundation is Jesus Christ our Lord'. I began pegging the napkins on the line, kicking the bowl along the ground with my foot until the whole line of them flapped like small triumphant flags in the breeze. I picked up the bowl feeling slightly guilty, like a small thief having pinched some sweeties from a jar. Never had it occured to me that I could be seen and every action examined by all the congregation in that Methodist Chapel. I had only to pop on the kettle for a well-earned cuppa, but it never had time to come to the boil. Into the kitchen marched Mrs Evans, her mouth screwed in a twisted, disapproving tight line and her head moving with such righteous indignation that the wide-brimmed hat moved with her in agitated jerks.

'There's nasty you are, after me telling you there was to be no washing on the line on Sunday, and 'tis wicked of you to be so defiant of God's laws. Six days shall you labour and do all your work. There's me sitting in my pew and everybody flabbergasted sitting there just watching you. I don't know how I shall lift my head up or explain to Reverend.'

Here she stopped for breath, but pointed down the garden to the offending terry squares brazenly flying high. Like an avenging angel covered with pious wrath, she stood there, with one white gloved hand pointing towards the line. I had no choice but to slink past her and retrieve the damp washing. Only when I had placed the bowl on the scullery table did she transfer a glare upon me that dared me in peril of my life to repeat this mortal Sabbath sin. Then with her head held high and the wide-brimmed hat flapping, she disappeared through the door. I made the cup of tea and sat down rather weakly after this outburst. Back at Kingswood, during my growing up years, we too had obediently gone to Chapel three times on Sunday, but soon drifted away when we were old enough to go to work and decide for ourselves. It was more a question of, as children do as you are told, later you can decide for yourself. Religion always taught you to fear The Lord. After Mrs Evan's little outburst, I felt slightly guilty, not about the washing on the line, but because I had caused her such trouble as to make her so upset. She had been very good to all of us so far. I wondered if it had been her honest belief that fire and brimstone might follow this ungodly action of mine, or was it because, as custodians of the church, their livelihood had been put in jeopardy by a foolish action on my part? I reasoned that if it was the latter, and of course it must be, I had every reason to feel mortified by my rash action, and resolved to apologise as soon as the opportunity arose. I also reasoned that it would be just as well if I made myself scarce for that day, at least. The Right Reverend would have cause to chastise them for allowing friends or visitors to break sacred laws. No doubt she would smart from this humiliation for some time. No, it would be unwise to be around today.

When John and Patty came down for breakfast, I enthused about the weather and was relieved when he suggested that we pay a visit to the Bosherton Lily Fields, a local beauty spot about five or six miles away. If we hurried, we could catch a bus that came along the high street at eleven o'clock. There was one that returned at four. We bustled around. With my small young family now, there seemed so many things to do and take with us, that we had to hurry in order to catch the bus. We made it at last, and relieved and relaxed, I sat in the bus with Patty by my side and Jacky on my lap, watching the lush green of the countryside speed by and loving the peace and magic of this part of the world. There were ruined castles on the side of the road, which Patty pointed to as 'funny houses', but which thrilled and delighted me and set my mind racing to the medieval days of the knights and ladies of the courts. The past was just a veil away and the story still in the stones as near and alive as ever.

Only a few other people alighted with us at our destination, right by the side of an old Saxon church. In

127

the silence of that perfect summer day, the years had done nothing to change or alter it. I would not have been at all surprised to hear the sound of horses' hooves on the highway, or to see a rider dismount, tether his horse and remove his headgear and walk reverently through the oak nail-studded door. I felt that I too had stood outside that same door many moons ago. Walking round the quiet graveyard that contained black tombs in a surround of rusty black iron spikes, I felt all of it was vaguely familiar.

I wanted to stay there, caught in that dream-like never-never land. All was silent save for the bees diving into the honey-sweet nectar of a bunch of clover growing by the side of the time-yellowed stone resting place, the inscription of who lay buried there long since erased. I was brought abruptly back to the present day by John insisting that we must hurry if we were to get everything in by four o'clock, and so followed him and Patty out of the church and along the road, vowing that I would come again one day to that sacred place.

Further on, we left the main road and entered a small wooded copse. The smell of rotting leaves, moss and pine needles came to us as we entered. High above us, we heard a frantic beating of wings and as we all looked upwards, a flock of birds, disturbed no doubt by our entry into their domain, rose up into the air with a great flurry of wings loudly protesting over the invasion of their privacy. We had to make our way cautiously, because the ground began to slope downward. I handed Jacky over to John; she was beginning to weigh heavily in my arms and I was glad of her release. She was wide awake. Her brilliantly blue eyes, so much like her Father's, were clear and shining. She smiled up at me as the exchange was being made. She was exquisite. Both children were beautiful. I stopped on the slippery muddy track to reach for her finger and to talk to her. Then we made our way carefully down the narrow track, going very slowly so that we could help Patty and prevent her from falling on the rough and dangerous incline. We breathed a sigh of relief when the bottom was finally reached and stood transfixed at the sight which met our gaze.

Twin lakes lay ahead of us, covered with creamy white and pink water lilies. A brick causeway, broken in places, ran between them and extended to the far side. The dark, dense, purpled woods on three sides formed a secluded, shrouded valley. Standing there in the haze, the lake shimmered and the lilies swayed lazily as bright emerald green and blue dragon flies darted from bloom to bloom. In this lake, it was said that King Arthur saw the hand holding the sword Excalibur rise and hold it aloft thrice. Here on that magical afternoon, if the whole court of King Arthur had appeared, I could have discredited nothing, Merlin with one wave had brought it all to life.

A couple of middle-aged ladies appeared from the wood and now stood beside us, looking at the causeway with some concern. Their eyes grew wide with fright when John picked Patty up and began to cross the crumbling, fragile path. Their frowns of distrust made it obvious that they had no intention of trusting themselves to it. Their looks turned to dismay when John returned and took Jacky from my arms to make yet another journey over the Causeway. I laughed when they actually covered their faces and turned away. I could hear their protests at our young foolhardiness. Yet I was caught and held in a spell of magic and safety. Only those who have ever ventured into this lovely hallowed spot can appreciate its beauty and its serenity. When I finally set out on the causeway to follow John, I stopped halfway to gaze into the lake, half wishing and all but convinced that the hand holding Excalibur could break the water and rise just for me. Believe that you have this thing, and you have it.

For all the brave pilgrims who finally made it to the other side, there was a tea shop run by two sisters who specialized in delicious home made scones filled with apricot jam and cream, wiilt pots of welcome tea and wafer thin slices of bread and butter. You went in through a green painted door and there was a black latch on the door which, when you pressed down hard on it, made a bell tinkle. I don't know if the tea shop is still there, but the lily fields are and the ancient church by the side of the copse. A new and safer causeway has now been built. Nobody who visits this place can dispute its magical atmosphere. I went back with Patty forty years later and it seemed I had never gone away.

25 · *It's an Ill Wind*

It was a relief to arrive back and find that Mr and Mrs Evans had gone to visit friends. They did not return until very late, when we had already gone to bed. The following day, by the time I came downstairs, she was busy with the church cleaning. I was free to hang the washing on the line and to allow Patty to play in the garden. Jacky also was wheeled into the sunshine. Popping in and out of the scullery, I could keep an eye on both of them. John was back at the base. It would be several days before another precious day could be arranged for all of us to be together again.

It wasn't until later that evening that I came face to face with Mrs Evans. I could see that she was still peeved about the unfortunate episode and she found it difficult to meet my gaze. l launched in to my apology with such humble contrition that she was instantly convinced of my sincerity, and the stony look on her face softened. Leaning over, she touched the back of my hand as though to implore me not to go on.

'Well now, my lovely, we'll not say another word about

it, but as long as you remain under this roof, the Lord's day must be observed.'

Her smile was warm and genuine. I was glad I had made my peace with her. That afternoon she took us for a walk to show us the barracks where the RAF boys first came to be trained. This of course was before John had transferred to Air-Sea Rescue.

'Smart all those laddies were, marching out of the barracks and all through the town. Proud we were too, standing there watching them. Specially that young man of yours. Proud we were of him when our Christina first brought him to our house.'

I looked at Mrs Evans, for it seemed her voice was conveying some far away picture that held a vague regret. I hoped she might reveal more, but the next moment she was back in the present again, looking at me and smiling.

'There now, my lovely, life plays and takes strange twists and tricks, and he's yours now with a family of two little girls. You have a good moral man as the father of those two babies, look you.'

Her voice trailed off a little and it seemed she was back again to some time in the past. Her head was turned away from me, but I caught the words, 'Our Christina was the loser — her and the boy.'

It was Wednesday before John was able to arrange another treat and to set off for Tenby, another seaside resort and another bus ride away. If there is any place that I would like to live and die in, it is Tenby. Like the rest of that part of Wales, its magic seemed to be every-where. Nothing would ever change. It seemed to convey this message wherever you went. Houses, shops, streets and hotels, all slumbered peacefully in an idyllic repose. You could nod on the beach or walk along the shore listening to the gurgle of baby waves breaking on the shingle, climb the hill to watch the boats bobbing in the harbour, but just as suddenly come upon some sacred spot filled with such energy that it would seem to come

131

alive to remind you of the past. Nowhere have I felt this more than all around this part of the coast.

At Saundersfoot, we spent one more perfect day. In fact, every time I close my eyes, I see again the twin lakes at Bosherton, the tiny boats bobbing in the harbour through the railings of the hotel on the hill at Tenby, the long stretch of golden sand at Saundersfoot mingled with the laughter of Patty and her Dad running in and out of the water and squealing as the tide filled and finally covered the castle he had built for her at the water's edge. Only one other place has been touched with such electrifying aliveness for me. There was a place in Ireland called Glendalock where the earliest Christian remains are reputed to be. There in a valley is a church and the remains of a monastery. This Brotherhood chose this beautiful spot to send out waves of love into a troubled world. Whilst I walked through the cemetery at Glendalock I looked through a Celtic cross and experienced the religious feeling of being caught in this great band of love which enveloped me and surrounded me. It was a love that surpassed all understanding. I knew that just so long as I stayed within that band of love, that nothing could hurt or harm me, and like the Celtic cross, there is no beginning and no end, but one complete circle into eternity. Wales was like that for me; like a religious experience. Coming so close to things that nothing was new, only hidden. Like a thin veil drawn over yesterday, but all is still there behind the veil.

A posting came for John the next day. Ironically, it was to be at a place called Trincomalee in Ceylon, where, but for the untimely event of War, we would have gone together in 1939. I was thinking of all this as I again packed the battered old black case. I said as much to Mrs Evans as she hugged me and wished me goodbye.

'Five years ago, I would have been going to that very place with him.'

'Five years ago, lovely, he might have been my son-in-law. All things turn out to be the best for somebody now,

132

look you.' Then she pulled me to her ample bosom and hugged me. She came to the gate and lifted the sagging piece of iron up by its middle and shifted it to one side so that we could pass through. 'One day, Mr Evans will get around to fixing the gate,' she laughed and waved us out of sight.

We waited on the same little halt station for the train. The scent of a musk rose came to me and a wasp buzzed angrily around John. He brushed it away. He was making funny exasperated faces, making Patty laugh, pretending to swish it away, saying, 'Go away, Mr Wasp, I'm not a ripe plum or strawberry jam, go away.' Then he ran to hide behind the bank of flowers and Patty laughed aloud at her father's comic antics. The train gave a very feminine whistle, unhurriedly slid into the station, and creaked to a gentle halt. John opened the carriage door and helped us in. He heaved the case up on to the rack, then handed me the holdall in which the spare nappies, the warm feed for Jacky and the square tin containing food for the journey were packed. He hugged Patty, telling her to be a good girl, then he kissed me and hoped that I had enjoyed the holiday. I nodded but could not find the words to tell him how I felt. The words and the pictures were all locked away inside my head. If he had laughed they would have been all blown away. They were in a secret place deep down inside, a place that I knew that John would have liked to unlock, and wouldn't be content until he was part of. There are things that should remain secret, things that make you remain yourself. 'Goodbye John,' I said, and kissed him. Then the train gave a little jolt and began to move slowly out of the tiny halt station; I looked at the white painted seat and whispered, 'Goodbye Pembrokeshire, goodbye Wales.'

For after so much beauty, how could anyone go home willingly?

26 · *The War Ends*

After the wide open spaces of Pembrokeshire, Repton Road seemed narrow and cramped. I felt I wanted to push the walls of the house outward so that these dark terraced houses could receive the light from the sun. All through that bitterly cold winter of 1944–45, it was only the dream of a home in the country that kept me going. High winds sent clouds of smoke down the chimney and the thick smoke and dust threatened almost to choke us to death; draughts crept under doors and through windows that rattled and shook so much we had to wedge them. I nursed the children through endless colds, coughs and sneezes, sitting up half the night with sips of hot lemon and cough mixture and trying desperately to cope with fetching and carrying coal and toddlers up and down the flight of stairs. In the spring, Patty went to school for the first time. She didn't seem to mind going to school, certainly she made no fuss. She enjoyed the games they played and the activity of the play area. But I became worried when I noticed that she did not mix in with the other children when they played, but preferred to stand and watch. When I took Jacky to collect her at tea time, she was always waiting for us to appear. I hoped that eventually she might adjust and find a friend. In other respects, she was a bright, average little girl. Early days, I thought, give her time.

Jacky's character was different to her sister's. She was a super-sensitive child, although it was some time before this fact was brought home to me. Too many harsh patches in my own life for me to cope with gave me little time to analyse Jacky's complex nature. She could be good for long spells at a time, but suddenly, without warning, she would burst into tears. The sobbing would continue for long periods. She was inconsolable, no amount of coaxing, loving or any other method could

Joyce with Jacky and Pat at the end of 1944

extract the cause. Anger at my own inadequacy, and a sharp note in my voice was enough to send her once more into hysterical sobbing. At this point, I could feel her lack of communication and want to love her more because of it. All attempts at appeasement were met with stiff limbs and an arched back. I suffered from guilt but struggled on, my own loveless upbringing demanded always that I get up and go on again.

That same year that Patty started school, the war ended. It had lasted for six long weary years, and for those of us who had been young at that time, it was a big slice out of our lives. When it was finally all over, there was singing and dancing in the streets. Victory bells rang and people cried and laughed at the same time and hugged each other. We had street parties for the children, and although they were too young to know what it was all about, they caught the excitement of the moment, and

135

with balloons and streamers they joined in the fun. I made sponges and jellies along with Jean Brodie from down the road, and even helped with the paper hats.

News filtered through that the war had ended suddenly because a small bomb had been dropped on Hiroshima. Nobody questioned why it had come to an abrupt halt. Like thousands of others, we were relieved and happy that hostilities had ceased and hoped that our lives could proceed along normal lines once more. It was several months before the word atomic was mentioned, and we were ignorant of its consequences. We ignored it all. The war was over and that was enough. Much later, we saw and heard the full horror of this weapon that the Americans had used and were appalled. That it must never happen again was a phrase that Governments bandied about for years, and which we believed, like so many other things. We were young and we were gullible. Impossible to think, then, that nuclear weapons would become the ultimate 'deterrent'. Impossible also to believe that when the final page of history was being written, we discovered that Germany had also been busy perfecting this deadly weapon of destruction, and it could have been us and not Hiroshima as the target. A moment for reflection. One sobering thought. How could things ever be the same again?

The men from the Forces came slowly back. They were welcomed home with bunting that stretched across the road from house to house. The parties started again, but this time in the houses themselves. Every one of the neighbours contributed to the meal, and people filed in and out to drink the health of the man who had returned and to receive a hug. John did not return with that first contingent of men — the spring and the summer of that year would pass into late autumn before he was released. Besides, John was a regular, and I was under the impression that he would want to stay in the Services and make it a career. Life for me resumed its grey day-to-day pattern. My mother-in-law was childishly hopeful and optimistic that everything would all come right in the end.

'I pray every night,' she said, simply, as though she and the Lord had some kind of understanding. Gertie would give one of her hyena-like laughs and say, 'Ma's at it again,' or some other similar comment. These two, so totally different in character, made a comedy act I could always be amused by. Even Emmy's disappearance every time she heard Gertie's voice only added to the absurdity of it all. Through it all, the kids were happy being Nana's little treasures and being spoilt by them all. They didn't mind Nan rummaging in her big black bag for snuffy chocolate, even my tut-tutting only made her laugh the more. That old house may have been dark and draughty, but it was never miserable. Her son was still her Darling Bertie, and his two daughters were her Darling Girls.

One Saturday afternoon, I took the girls shopping with me down to Sandy Park. I needed some things for the weekend and most especially some bread. I stopped by the cake shop and pulled the pushchair with Jacky in it to the side telling Pat to keep an eye on her sister. Jacky began to arch her back in a series of gymnastic jerks, an early indication that she wanted something. I held my breath and counted to ten, then patiently attempted to extract from her exactly what it was she wanted.

'A groosebery in a pot,' Jacky said and perversely covered her face with both hands.

'What,' I said, trying to stay calm, 'is a groosebery in a pot?' Patty was skipping about on one foot. She did not know what it was and shook her head. Jackie began another series of strainings at the harness that kept her in the pushchair, and in desperation I unstrapped her and pulled her into the shop. In another moment, I knew she would burst into tears and this would make me feel inadequate and guilty. It wasn't always easy to know what an eighteen month old child wanted. The green-coated assistant looked curiously at Jacky and several customers tried in vain to help. Was it an iced bun that she wanted, or perhaps the jam doughnut? A small crowd of middle-aged women twittered around Jacky, trying to coax her into telling them what it was she wanted. All she did was shake her head vigorously from side to side and slip prostrate on the floor. I gave a despairing look at the assistant and prepared to scoop up my supine infant from the floor and escape into the street. Suddenly the counter hand reached forward to take a solitary cake, forlornly left on the shining glass window display. With a triumphant cry, she addressed the back of my infant's head, which was pathetically buried beneath the pillow of her pushchair, where I had unceremoniously dumped her to make my hasty retreat.

'This is what she wants, isn't it dear?' our Samaritan from behind the counter said soothingly. 'Your Nana buys you one of these every week when she comes in for her bread.'

The pastry was in the shape of a small cup and filled with gooseberries and a small blob of cream on the top. A groosebery in a pot. The mystery was solved. Jacky sat up obediently and took the proffered gooseberry tart. The tears still glistened in those big baby blue eyes. The middle-aged fond Grannies simultaneously murmured,

'Ah, bless her little heart.'

I wheeled Jacky, happily nibbling at the cake, oblivious to the fact that the crumbs were falling down the front of her clean coat, out into the street once more. I felt as though I had been unjust and unkind. More patience and diplomacy may have averted the scene. We seemed always to reach a point where the sparks would fly, yet I always felt guilty when she was reduced to this helpless state. I was still trying to fathom out my inadequacies, when I realised that I had not offered Patty a cake. Patty was happily skipping along by my side. She wasn't bothered, but it was one more thing for me to worry about.

Minnie was in a twitter of excitement when we arrived back at the house. There had been a telegram for me whilst I was out. It was just one short line to say John was arriving home the next day approx 10:30 please meet.

'Your Daddy is coming home my Pet,' Nan Storey was saying to Jacky, bending down and rubbing her chubby little knees.

'Tomorrow you are going down to the station to see your Dad come home on a chuff-chuff.'

I made a face at this expression, and Jacky shook her head obstinately and said stubbornly, 'No, swings.' I groaned. Not another battle, please God. The rest of the evening was a mad rush to find and get ready clean dresses for the girls. It would mean an early rise if I had to get to the station for ten-thirty in the morning. I had recently bought the girls matching blue skirts and tops with animal motifs on the blouses. I decided these would be appropriate for the weather. Pat was ready first. At five she was independent and also a help to me. Jacky was having a tussle with me over the top, that was needing to be stretched a little to go over her head, the seconds were ticking past, and I had no time to play games. I gave the top a quick jerk down over her head and pushed her arms through the sleeves. Jacky screamed that the top was itchy and began to arch her back in preparation for another disapproving act. I shouted to Pat to go and stand by the door, to be ready for when I had finished the tussle with Jacky. I did not want to face the floods of tears so I yanked off the offending top and allowed her to wear a blouse from a pile of grubby unwashed things. I buttoned up her shoes and pushed her through the passage, and through the gate, there to be confronted with Patty talking to her father in the friendliest terms. His kit bag had been placed on the wall and he was deep in conversation with his daughter.

'Chuff-chuff,' Jacky said imperiously, tugging at my hand and pulling me away from the rather startled gaze of John. Patty looked up at her father endeavouring to clarify the situation by explaining gravely,

'If she doesn't go for a walk, she will only play Mummy

139

up and Mummy promised her the trains and the swings.'
We all stood there, uncertain of our next move, with
Jacky threatening to throw herself prostrate onto the
pavement if her demands were not met. John made the
first move.

'Tell you what,' he said, 'I'll dump the kitbag, and we'll
all go to the park with Jacky on the swings. It will give us
an appetite for our dinner.'

When he came out of the house a few minutes later,
the two girls ran ahead, and we walked slowly on behind.
I was suddenly at a loss to know what to say. He looked
at me and his only comment was, 'Well I never — well I
never did.'

27 · *When Johnny Comes Marching Home Again*

John found it difficult to settle. In our cramped surroundings, the tiny bedroom and lack of space and
privacy stifled him. He was used to the great outdoor life
with male companions, all thrown together in a common
cause. He was irritable, and the pub once again became
the focal point for social contact and the great escape.

I did not improve matters by choosing this rather
fraught period to insist that we talk about some form of
family planning. This news, delivered one morning
at the breakfast table, was met with quiet but hostile
pomposity.

'My dear,' he said whilst reaching for the cornflakes, 'I
am not the giver of life or death, and whether you have
one child or fifty makes not the slightest difference to
me. If you don't want any more children, then you must
do something about it and not I.'

Once again I felt angry and resentful. I would have

shrunk from going into a chemist's shop to ask for any contraceptive aid, even if I knew what to ask for. Men had a secret system of nods and winks, they could emerge from the shop cheerfully whistling, 'there's a good time coming', but no self-respecting girl would even think about such a thing. Modesty decreed that a man knew all these things and women should not. And I did not know where to turn or who to ask for advice.

Very, very slowly, rubble was being cleared and a new building programme was underway. The Council acquired land in semi-rural areas on the outskirts of the city, and big estates began to be developed. Builders were asked to submit tenders for cheap rented dwellings, and soon names like Laings, Willerby and Stone began to appear on huge hoardings. A Housing Committee was set up to deal with the thousands and thousands of applicants who rushed to add their names to the formidable list already there.

A prefab was the desire and love of my life. These consisted of prefabricated pieces, mass produced in sections, loaded onto lorries, and taken to a site where they could be assembled almost overnight. They were delightful chalet-type little dwellings, made of some kind of asbestos. Although it was thought they would only last ten years, they did enable many thousands of people to be rehoused quickly, and they were firm favourites because of their compactness and ultra-modern design. The kitchen housed a number of labour-saving units, including a stove and a fridge along one wall, together with cupboard space and a delightful alcove for the breakfast area. In the lounge, windows which extended from the front round to the side, gave light and brightness. The fire was an all-night Rayburn and provided warm air to the other two rooms through vents in the wall. Finally, a large airing cupboard in the hall was also heated by the master fire and when the doors were left open, the hall would be warm and cosy too. A large garden front and back was also a feature that appealed

141

to me. Over the cute little porch, I could picture roses and honeysuckle. I wanted one of those prefabs more than anything else in the world.

We all made trips to the Housing Committee, foolishly thinking that by harassing them we would get a house all that much quicker. We were allocated points, according to our circumstances, and those who could wangle a few extra points by stating special hardship got in there first. Some people even applied to local councillors to further their cause. A lot of good work was done at that time by caring local representatives who knew how desperate people were to be decently rehoused.

With all this rehousing going on, there was a tremendous demand for furniture. We'd had to make do and mend all through the war, but rationing did not stop with the coming of peace, for raw materials were still in short supply. The new furniture coming into the shops was Utility, and conformed to the Government's guidelines on manufacture. The Utility bedroom, kitchen and dining suites were good solid stuff, not much style, but it was cheap, durable and came in three choices of wood finish — pine, oak or mahogany. Shops did a roaring trade. Most young people ordered suites and started paying for them long before any news of a house of their own was remotely possible. We dyed sheets for curtains because, as yet, there were no luxury goods available.

Jean Brodie came rushing over one Monday morning, brandishing a letter from the Housing to tell her that she had been allocated a prefab at Shirehampton. Her luck in getting one of these was due to having two children of the same sex. Any increase in her family would mean that she would have to apply for a three bedroomed dwelling. Prefabs had but two bedrooms, and were classed as temporary dwellings.

'You'll get one with your two girls,' she said excitedly. 'I told my Fred that all *his* energy would have to go on workin' 'ard to buy a few bits and bobs for the new 'ouse, cos we ain't got nuthin.' She nudged me and said with a wink, 'Tell yore ol' man to tie a knot in it!'

Here was my chance to extract any secret knowledge that she could impart to me. 'Getting off at Crewe' had already been tried without much success; it made us both irritable, and it was unreliable. In the next few moments, I gathered from her that she used a product called Rendalls. These were small, round pessaries of a soap-like substance. To quote Jean's delightfully quaint description,

'Shove 'em up as far as they'll go and wait till they fizz!' She rushed back over the road to get a couple that were left in the box for me to try.

Jean omitted to tell me that the effervescent period was limited, or maybe time had rendered their effectiveness to nil. Whatever the reason, they did not work for me and, a few weeks later, I found myself once again experiencing the joys of early pregnancy by being revoltingly sick and irritable.

My dream of a prefab was shattered. I went to see Jean in her new home and howled, even while enthusing about the way she had transformed her little home and planted grass in the front for a lawn. A young sapling by the front gate would soon spread its foliage over the path, attractive and inviting. It wasn't fair. I wanted a home like this, and once more I was being denied it. Jean commiserated.

'Take a load of Beecham's pills, have a mustard bath, drink lots of gin, move all the furniture, mangle a wet blanket.'

I tried it all and nothing worked. Then Jean offered a ray of hope. She said that if I went to the doctor and convinced him that having another baby would prove detrimental to my health, both mentally and physically, he might just agree to terminate the pregnancy.

'Squeeze a few tears out,' I was advised.

The tears were genuine and I was shedding them unashamedly, when I became aware that the doctor was scribbling something on paper and had never once lifted his eyes to look directly at me. Eventually, completely unmoved by my sad saga, he coolly remarked that he was unable to help me, but that he would refer me to a gynaecologist who, in his opinion, I ought to see.

Filled with doubt but still hoping, a couple of weeks later I walked into the clinical purity of the consulting room of the great woman, who surveyed me quizzically like some rare germ under the microscope. It was obvious that her views coincided exactly with those of her male counterpart.

'Mrs Storey,' she said at last, 'what you are asking me to do amounts to murder.'

My eyes looked back at her pale ones in defiance. 'So is War,' l said, 'plus the little known fact that as many women die in childbirth as there are casualties in a war.'

Her eyes did not rise from the papers on her desk. It was not lost on me that she was choosing deliberately to ignore my remark and to dismiss it as the ravings of a demented soul.

'As far as I'm concerned, you are going to have a baby, and that is precisely what you will go home to do. Should any foolish action of yours bring about an abortion, may I point out to you that you are liable to prosecution? I shall write to your husband to make sure that he, too, is in possession of the facts.'

There were not many choices for us in those days, and choice means freedom. The winds of change did not blow early enough for me, and I am glad that time dealt more kindly with my three girls. That same woman who sent me away feeling desperate, smilingly invited my own daughter into her waiting room to arrange a termination as a matter of course twenty-odd years later.

28 · *Love and Misses*

This was a period when men were trying to adjust to rebuilding severed relationships and establishing their place in a strange, changed world. John found himself a job with a construction works making bus engines, but found a nine to five job boring and restrictive. He changed his job and became a conductor on the buses. He still hated the early morning shifts and the unsociable hours, and I found it difficult to keep the children quiet when he was trying to sleep. I decided to write to our Councillor for an appointment. I was writing the letter, sitting at the table in the window, when I saw big brother Den come in at the gate. I rapped at the glass to attract his attention and he looked up and saw me and waved. I was four months pregnant. I went rushing down the stairs to let him in, tearing off my pinny and throwing it on the hall stand as I went. I wore that damned thing twenty-four hours a day it seemed! Den stood there on the doorstep looking brown and happy, and I threw my arms about his neck and drew him into the hall. Arm-in-arm, we went through into the kitchen for me to put the kettle on — I wanted to know everything that had happened to him since the last time we had met.

All the time I'd been in Grimsby, my mother had only written to me once, and she had never visited me. Den, on the other hand, had written regularly so I knew that he had met his wife-to-be, Audrey, when he'd been based in Staffordshire. Audrey worked in the NAAFI, and she and Den were married in Burton-on-Trent. My parents had gone up for the wedding. Den told me that he and Audrey were now living with George and Ada in Burchell's Green Road, and added that the real reason for his visit was to find out how many points I had towards a house. I gathered from his conversation that things were not easy living with Ada and George,

145

especially now that Audrey was pregnant. Ada found fault with everything Audrey did. I brought in some cups and saucers on a tray, and a big pot of tea. I pulled up a couple of chairs, and went in search of milk and the biscuit barrel. I poured out the tea, then, without looking, went to sit down on the chair that I had just pulled out for myself. To my surprise, it wasn't there and I fell heavily back on the bar of the brass fender round the grate. I experienced a sharp pain, but it was soon gone, and Den was helping me to my feet, looking concerned and contrite, saying he had pushed the chair away because it was in a direct line with the door, and he wanted to give me enough space when I came in with the milk and biscuits. He was surprised I had not seen what he had done; he was very upset and kept asking me if I was sure I had not hurt myself.

'Come on, tell me the rest of your news. Of course I'm alright.'

As he had no children, he hoped Audrey's pregnancy might make a difference to their chances of getting a house. He was surprised I was not already housed, and it came as a shock to realise that I had been married for eight years, and during that time we, and thousands like us, had never had a house of our own.

Den began to talk about the war and his bomber raids over Germany. As I sat there and listened to him, I was amazed that he had chosen as dangerous a job as rear-gunner in this war. He was such a gentle person. I remembered him as the anything-for-a-quiet-life brother, who had elected to stay locked in that front room at South Road to be as far away as possible from the bickering that went on in the rest of the house all the time. Why, of all things, had he chosen Bomber Command?

'Well,' he said, 'I was in the RAF from 1940, as you know. One day, in the Spring of 1942, I was visiting a friend in Canterbury, and there was a massive air raid. We took shelter under the stairs for a couple of hours whilst it lasted. Canterbury was pounded by thousands

146

Dennis Dark (right) with mate, around 1943

and thousands of incendiaries. The centre was a dreadful sight; the Cathedral was still standing, but great holes had appeared in the green precinct, and the stonework had been badly scarred. I was surprised to see great gaps in the row of houses where we had sheltered. As I took in the scene a great wave of anger and frustration crept over me. If I could only hit back! Here was a lovely city which up till then had survived intact — it just made me so mad.' He spread his hands in a helpless gesture. 'So the first thing I decided to do when I returned to my unit was to ask for a transfer to Bomber Command, and in due course I was accepted for training as air crew. A new Head had just been appointed — "Bomber" Harris we called him — who felt that intensive, massive bombing of Germany could win the war.'

He stirred his tea, and stared into the distance, alone with his own thoughts. Without being told, I knew what he was thinking about: all those thousands of young men who would never come back.

'At the end of the war, I managed to get a flight over Germany, you know. I saw for myself the devastation of industry and the cities in the Ruhr, and I never dreamed that such destruction could have been inflicted. I saw the awful mess that had been made of Cologne and Essen, and wondered what the German people felt toward Hitler, who had sown the seeds of their destruction.'

'Tell me about your Distinguished Flying Medal.' I was full of curiosity.

'Oh, it wasn't just me, you know. . . .' He was embarrassed. 'I just spotted an enemy fighter, and we took evasive action and . . . Look, it was a team effort, all of us in it together, nothing especially heroic. Something I shall never forget, though, was being decorated by the King. It was a very great honour and a moment I shall treasure all my life. I felt so proud.'

He smiled and took another sip of his tea. Looking at him, I felt that I was seeing him for the first time in my life and I too, felt proud to have such a man for my brother.

148

29 · *A Miscarriage*

I had been to the park with Jacky. Afterwards I collected Pat from school and was pushing the pram through the front door, when I felt hot and very dizzy. I sat on the bottom step of the stairs, shooing both girls up to the bedroom and telling them to play until I could come up to get them their tea. Presently the faintness passed and I tried unsuccessfully to wedge the now folded up pushchair into the tiny space behind the glass door. Something seemed to be blocking the way and with annoyance I jabbed the thing viciously forward, scraping the hood along the wall so hard that I dislodged one of the protective corner bits and it fell with a tiny metallic click on to the floor. As I bent to feel for it, there was a loud singing in my head and a wave of sickness swept over me. I just had time to rush outside to the loo when a great blackness came over me and I knew nothing more.

When I came round a few seconds later, I was sitting with my back propped up against the wooden post of the door. Age had rendered this old door post unsafe, and with my added weight falling against it, the rotting wood had been pulled from its foundation and was now snapped off at the base. Dozens of woodlice were crawling around in all directions, as, deprived of a home, they sought new surroundings. Some were making a detour over me. I shivered, not from disgust, but from a lowered body temperature after the fainting attack. I felt cold and very ill. I rose unsteadily to my feet. My head swam and I thought I would faint again. I crawled on my hands and knees to the stairs. The top seemed a million miles away. There was nobody about. Gertie was not home from work and my mother-in-law was at Gwen's. John was on the late shift. When I finally made it to the big double bed, I lay there for a long while with my face

149

into the pillow fighting the black waves of sick faintness that swept over me.

From a long way off I heard Gertie call out from the bottom of the stairs,

'Anyone alive in this joint?'

Both the children rushed down the stairs to greet her. I knew but didn't care that she would be stuffing them with the cakes and sweets that she brought home for them every night. I lay face downward for a long time. Deep inside, I felt a tiny 'pop' like the bursting of a pea pod and something wet and sticky around the top of my legs. Then pain like I had never experienced before took my breath away, enveloping me so that relief came only with blackness, and I floated away. Muffled voices came and went.

'Be you alright?'

Somebody groaned, 'Oh my God.'

I was dancing again on Pagan Hill. Pagan Hill was a favourite walk where the two young Nurses brought us on sunny afternoons, way, way back at Painswick when I was a small child. They often told us stories of how the witches danced in the magic ring on halloween on Pagan Hill, calling on Diana, their queen, to come at midnight to grant them a wish.

'You'll frit the life out of those kids,' Nurse Hester, the older nurse, used to say. They had been amused that day when I had taken off my shoes and socks to run barefoot onto the grass to dance. They had clapped and clapped to encourage the mad twirls and swirls. Polly didn't scare me, not even when she began to recite something about calling on Diana and Hester gave her a very angry look.

'Will she really, really come if I call her on Halloween?'

'The magic is in the believing,' Polly had told me.

I was going to ask Diana to send my Mother to see me. No-one had come that night in Painswick. Perhaps I had not believed hard enough.

I was dancing again on Pagan Hill. The grass was emerald green and I was as light as air. The sky

150

was bright with stars and I heard a bell ring. Bells in Switzerland. I felt a rush of wind and heard a sound like the wheels of a train clacking on the lines as it passed through a tunnel, but there were lights that suspended, hurt my eyes. As I rushed past them, I saw Diana's face float close to mine. She wore her lovely dark hair piled high on top of her head with a white crown holding it in place. She should let it fall loose round her shoulders just like a mantle, black and shining in the wind. She bent over me and took hold of my hand. She was very beautiful. I tried to say,

'I knew you would come,' but she was fading away and a loud male voice shouted,

'Make way for the suicide case.'

How very sad, I thought, someone had committed suicide, but what had that to do with me? Nothing at all. Voices now, fading, then coming.

'Can you hear me?'

'Will you open your eyes please, we have to take some particulars.'

I struggled desperately to open my eyes. I wanted to see Diana again, but instead I saw the uniformed figure of a nurse standing by my side. On the bibbed front of her pristine white starched apron was a vermilion stain. I was lying on a red sheet, the same colour as the crimson slashes on the white uniform, except that the sheet was wet and shiny, the colour of blood. There was blood everywhere. There was something else on that crimson sheet. Something so small, so perfect in its compactness, that I felt a sense of utter loss and pity and began to sob uncontrollably. With grim faces, they wheeled me into a brightly lit delivery room to clean me up and to remove that fragile, miniature, lifeless form, that filled me with such sorrow and anguish.

The following morning, I was awakened by the sounds of an all too familiar routine, and just for the moment, I thought I was back at the Nunsthorpe Maternity Home. Beds and lockers were being pulled aside in order to

151

be swept and polished to a high degree of brightness. Flowers that had been taken out of the ward the night before now graced the window sills and lockers. Beds were straightened and patients washed and groomed now sat up in their beds with an air of quiet expectancy. The reason for all this spit and polish was the daily round of the doctor, and in this, matron had an important role to play. With her starched head square that formed part of her uniform standing out stiffly behind her, she now stood by the first patient's bed at the top of the ward. She had already taken the case history from the clipboard at the bottom of the bed. This she would hand to the doctor as soon as he came through the door and advanced to her side. Through the window, an impudent sunbeam caught and held the whirling specks of dust that had been disturbed, dancing and glinting in that long shaft of sunlight. It seemed almost an act of wilful insubordination in all this clinical sterility. Matron's headpiece crackled with starched brittleness as she turned her head to smile at the great man who, with a retinue of students, came through the door at that precise moment.

I lay there passively watching the small procession move slowly along the ward. Apart from a first eye-catching 'Good Morning' to the patient, or 'How are we this morning?', any other discussion about the patient's condition was delivered solely to the students who hung around in a small circle at the bottom of the bed, out of reach and sound of the person whom it concerned. They held the view that what you didn't know about you couldn't worry about.

'It wouldn't matter in my case,' I thought grimly, 'everybody already knows about me.' Only that morning, I had heard the woman in the bed opposite whisper loudly to her neighbour.

'I've been waiting five years for a baby, and she gets rid of hers.'

Can I be blamed for her infertility? I thought resentfully. Yet there was something in my easy fertility that

152

angered her and made her so hostile to me. Her child-lessness made her a woman to be pitied, my effortless conception earned me the sneering title 'a good little breeder'. I wished I had more control over my life. This feeling of inadequacy almost made me throw abuse back at her: What has your wretched life to do with me, why do I have to carry your guilt as well as my own? I knew even as I lay there that we all belonged to that sad band of women who, like our mothers before us, had all asked that same question—'Why me?'

When the small party reached my bed, I opened my eyes to receive the customary greeting, even stretching my mouth into a semblance of a smile. After all, being polite didn't cost much, and sometimes turned the tide. But both matron and the doctor kept their eyes averted. No greeting for me and, feeling more like a leper than ever, I slid back against the pillows and endeavoured to slide as far as possible down into the bed and out of sight. I felt a slight indentation at the bottom of the bed and surmised that someone was sitting there. I kept my eyes closed tight and heard a man's voice commanding sternly,

'Mrs Storey, have you any idea how this could have happened?'

I chose not to answer. His voice was loud enough for the whole ward to have every ear inclined and every muscle tensed to hear this interrogation and to await the outcome. Through the grapevine of the medical staff, from the gynaecologist to the trainee nurse, would have gone the saga of my previous visit and request for a termination of a pregnancy. Oh wicked, wicked woman, in the eyes of the church and of God what mortal sin had I committed? Sackcloth and ashes and the wearing of them for the rest of my life would never atone. Once more the question was repeated and once more, I could not speak one word in my own defence. In sheer desperation, I covered my head with the bedcovers. I felt the weight on the end of my bed lift suddenly and a

153

lighter weight thrown on to it. I guessed that it was my case history that had been thrown with anger on my bed. This convinced me that they had all washed their hands of me. In defiance and frustration, I moved my foot in the bed and dislodged the sheaf of white paper held so securely together on its metal clipboard and sent it crashing to the ground. Only a couple of the patients gave a slight start as they watched every move of the proceedings; the doctor and his entourage continued on their way. They gave not a hint that anything was amiss or that they had even seen what happened, and when the final patient had been saluted and checked, matron rustled and creaked to the door and disappeared with the doctor through the great swing doors.

At seven o'clock that night, the first visitors began to arrive. I watched them coming in, all bearing gifts. Lockers were being opened to house goodies that could be eaten later. Flowers were held aloft for fellow patients to admire. Chairs scraped near to beds, hands were held and intimate low toned whispers came to me as I lay there waiting for John to appear through the door. Tearful and sad, I waited to be reassured and consoled. More than anything else, I needed a shoulder to cry on. I watched the door, for it seemed that John was a long time putting in an appearance. When he did at last come through the door, there was no welcoming smile on his face and when he bent to kiss me, I saw his eyes were wet with tears. Very foolishly, I thought his tears conveyed concern for me and I was about to hasten to reassure him that I was alright. When he spoke, his voice was gruff with actual emotion so that when his words finally sank in, they were like a physical body blow,

'I have just been informed that the child you aborted last night was a boy. You have murdered my son.'

I was drowning again and I hurt.

30 · *Sent to Coventry*

For the whole of the three days that I was there, nobody spoke to me and my misery was complete. I was frozen inside and prayed that I might never feel anything again, neither love nor hate. In fact, I began to feel that I was two people. One was quietly watching from the safety of being enclosed, observing and taking everything in but never being hurt. When anger made it imperative for me to make a stand, the knowledge that I had defected in some way and would have to start all over again always upset me more than the actual reason for the anger.

They dismissed me on the third day. Before I went, I had to see the almoner, who told me that I would be charged ten pounds for my short stay at Bristol General Hospital. I could pay it all at once, or in the case of extreme hardship, in three monthly instalments. I chose the latter, knowing that would be equally as difficult to pay out of John's meagre wages. She then said that she could arrange a taxi for transport home, but I brushed that suggestion aside. I had no money for a taxi. Without looking up from the ledger in which she was writing, she informed me that I could wait for the ambulance, but as they were busy in the mornings, it might be late after-noon before one was available to take me home. On the spur of the moment, I made the rash statement that I would wait for neither and that I would walk home. I had reason to regret this far too hasty decision, long before I had got even half way there.

I walked down the steps of the hospital and out into the street. After the warmth of the ward, the keen October wind felt cold. I made my way along York Road and out towards Temple Meads, stopping several times because of my weakened condition. Walking along the Netham and on towards Newbridge Road, I stood for a long time watching the river and remembering when, as children, we were taken up to Beese's Tea Gardens in the barge. Every Whitsuntide this was a great treat that we looked forward to with such eager anticipation. The old barge on the other side of the bank was solitary and empty now. Its dirty black hulk periodically bumped the side of the bank with dismal thuds when the fast flowing tide tugged at its rope moorings. As I stood there, deep in thoughts of the past, the sad little poem we once learned at school came into my mind.

Willows whiten, aspens quiver-
Little wavelets dusk and shiver-
In an island in the river
Going down to Camelot.

I shivered. I was glad I was on the last lap of my journey now. The short cut along Whitby Road and past the Co-op Dairy would bring me into Sandy Park and Repton Road. All I could think of now was that big bed and a long, long sleep. I pushed my hand through the letterbox. The key was on the end of a long piece of string, all I had to do was to pull it through and insert it in the lock. There was nobody at home and when I had wearily climbed the stairs, the bedroom was full of children's muddles and the bed was unmade. I took off my coat and threw it onto a chair that was already half submerged with clothes and books. Not caring very much, and longing for a cup of tea, I debated whether I would descend all those steps again just to fill the blasted kettle. In the end, I decided against it. It was too much of an effort. This simple fact made me feel irritable and weepy, so I got into the unmade bed and was asleep in no time at all.

I dreamed I was watching a beautiful white horse galloping wild and free along a sandy shore line. When it came to a halt by a formation of rocks, it shook its long flowing mane and pawed at the ground. In the moonlight, standing there silhouetted against the skyline, that graceful form seemed to be filled with the sheer joy of living.

156

From behind a rock I became aware of a man creeping quietly forward towards the horse. In his hand, he held a bridle and bit. He was gently coaxing the horse, talking to it and edging nearer and nearer. I watched the two of them intently. I saw the head of the horse jerk up as it sensed the danger. Then it shied away, just as the man was about to throw the bridle over my horse's neck. I was glad when I heard its hooves thudding away into the distance. The man was not perturbed. He would try again tomorrow.

When I opened my eyes, the two girls were clambering all over me and snuggling down one on each side of me. 'Mummy's home' they kept repeating.

'Why didn't you let me know you were coming home today, I would have come to fetch you?' John was bending over the small round gas ring in the grate when he asked the question. I watched him strike a match and saw the ring of blue flame flare up, then it was covered by the kettle and the thought of a welcome cuppa made me feel good. I settled back against the pillows with the children, and watched him performing these small domestic tasks. John was good at playing with the girls. He played the role of Mr Dragon, who snapped up Jacky's bread and jam when she wasn't looking so that she had to eat it up quick before Mr Dragon got there. Much later, when they were ready for bed, he told them a made up story about how, when the wind blew, all the little men would shake the stalks of the long grass to make it bend this way and that.

The wind actually was whipping up outside and making the windows rattle. After a while I got quite irritated with the noise. Once again I looked around this pathetic little shambles of a room that we all shared as both living room and bedroom. A well known cliche came to me: 'Start off with nowt, always have nowt'.

'For God's sake put a bloody wedge in that window,' I yelled at John, and was surprised at the anger that welled up from so deep inside me. He looked up, startled at my

157

outburst, but got up and obediently wedged the window and pulled the curtains. After a while, the small glow from the fire, along with the rise and fall of the children's breathing, softened the room and I fell asleep again long before John came to bed. Occasionally, the light from the headlamps of a car or motor bike would circle the room and leave long shadows on the wall, then the room and the road would be silent and dark once again.

The following morning I was awakened by John shaking my shoulder. I was surprised to find that he had already taken Pat to school. Jacky was demanding that she be taken to the swings. The unlit fire, the unmade beds, and the pile of unwashed crocks, all added to the general squalor of the room. I listened to John's voice, not fully comprehending at first what he was trying to convey. The good-natured banter of the night before had vanished, and in its place was a kind of whine that indicated his patience was wearing thin.

'Will there be any dinner for me tonight when I come in?'

I thought dully, what does he mean? Wasn't there always a dinner on the table for him, whatever time he chose to eat it? I continued to blink and to stare back at him. He mistook the silence and the stare for insolence and continued angrily.

'Look, I can't take any more time off from work. You are home now and have all day to rest if you want to. I will take a few bob from your housekeeping to buy my dinner at the canteen, that way you will only need to see to the kids and yourself.'

I watched him take the money from my purse and then heard his footsteps clattering down the stairs. The door slammed so hard that the knocker at the top of the door gave an extra angry little ratatat. I surveyed the room with dislike and distaste. From the grey embers in the grate, to Jacky, who had squatted herself on the floor and was displaying a bout of bad temper because she was being denied a visit to the swings.

'Shut up!' I yelled at her through clenched teeth. She was so surprised that just for a second she sat there with her mouth wide open, then with a renewed vigour she let rip again. I sat and watched her. As far as I was concerned she could howl all day, getting up to restore the room to some kind of order would be more than I could cope with. Miss Jacky's tantrums were her affair and the sooner she learned I was not there for her special benefit, the better for all of us.

'Who's being murdered up there?' Gertie's good-natured and strident voice came from the bottom of the stairs.

'None of your business!' I shouted back, then sat bolt upright in bed. What was the matter with me, wanting to strike out at everyone in sight? Some little demon leaped out from inside me on the slightest provocation. 'Get up, go on again' my mother would have said, but my little demon answered,

'What the hell for, you silly cow.'

Gertie opened the door very gingerly, because Jacky's bottom was behind it. She took in the situation and in her rough way tried to resolve it.

'Come on my babby,' she said coaxingly to Jacky. 'Come down the shops with Gertie.'

'Swings,' Jacky said defiantly and got up to take Gertie's hand and follow her down the stairs.

'Alright then,' Gertie replied, placating her and looking apologetically towards me. 'It'll give 'ee a bit of a rest,' she nodded and beamed. 'Shan't be mor'n half an hour.'

I didn't answer, but thought grimly she'd be all the morning if I knew Miss Jacky.

Again I closed my eyes, but now the untidiness of the room got on my nerves. Besides, I was thirsty enough to want to drink a gallon of tea. I rolled out of bed and began to dress. When I went to the recess to pull the curtains, I spotted the half finished letter that I had been writing to our councillor that morning when Den had paid me a visit. It was still in the pad, but as someone had

159

put a cup of tea on the front page, there was now a brown ringed stain obliterating the words. I sat down at the table and tore it all up.

I lit the fire and tidied the room. Made a pot of tea and again sat in the window sipping the brew and reflecting savagely on my beleaguered environment.

'Somebody ought to see the way I have to live.' I said the words aloud because I felt so desperate, and then once again it was anger that made me pick up the pen and write to the Council for an interview. Nobody had come as yet to assess us, or given us any points, and in that moment I decided I would fight for the right to live in better and healthier surroundings. I was going to make sure that I got a house or a prefab, even a caravan was better than all this. I walked to the post office and fixed the stamp. When I finally slipped it through the letter box, I heard it flop to the bottom.

'That is that,' I said and looked up at the sky. 'I've done my bit, now you do yours!'

A few days later I wrote another letter to the local councillor. I was going to leave no stone unturned this time. It was a week later that a man from the Housing came out to see me, and Ma had been primed to say that she couldn't stand the noise the children made and wanted the bedroom back, otherwise she would have to give us notice to quit. The man from the Housing thought this was a disgraceful thing for a mother to do.

'Would you really see your own flesh and blood put out into the street?' he demanded with his eyes bulging with disbelief. However, although we were quite high on the list for points, he could not say how early we would be housed. Incredible as it seems, there were a great many families living in worse conditions, with, for instance, damp walls and in some cases, bugs and infestation to contend with.

Everybody must fight for what they believe, in their own way. Being singleminded was my choice, so that when I received a reply from our local councillor granting

160

us both an interview for the following Monday evening, I pushed John out through the front door even before he'd had a chance to have a cup of tea. He grumbled about being done out of his grub right up to the gate of Reg Brown's house and as we rang the bell I hissed at him.

'You can have your blasted dinner and supper all in one when we get back!'

The two men chatted for an hour about the air-sea rescue that John had served in. Not once did he even mention me. I stifled a yawn as the conversation turned to gardening, and John was asked if this was a favourite hobby of his. John was wise enough to expand on this subject and declare that the loss of a garden was his one regret now that he was in civvy street. He said that if he was lucky enough to get a council house, he hoped it would be a corner house so that he would have extra garden to work at. Reg Brown leaned confidentially across at John and said earnestly,

'Yes, my son, work the garden, it will pay off dividends.'

On the way home, I asked John if what he had told Mr Brown was true.

'Do you really like gardening?'

'God no,' he replied quickly, 'a plot bigger than a postage stamp would kill me.'

31 · *Our First Home*

The miracle finally happened. One day I came down the stairs to find a long white official letter from the Housing Committee there on the mat.

'That your letter from the Housing?' Gertie enquired, coming out of the front room with a tray of dirty crocks and following me out into the kitchen. Minnie was drinking her third cup of tea that morning.

161

'Ma,' Gertie's shrill voice directed itself to mother-in-law, 'she's got her letter from the Housing.'

Minnie lifted both large hands to heaven, the right hand still holding a copious pinch of snuff.

'Oh, thank God,' she exclaimed piously. Then, opening one eye, she enquired, 'Where to, kid?'

I opened the letter and read: 'You have been allocated a house at 123 Ullswater Road, Southmead, at a rental of sixteen shillings a week, paid fortnightly in advance'.

'Absolutely ridiculous,' John exploded when he was informed about the house later that day. 'How in the world will I be able to afford that kind of money in advance?'

At that precise moment, I felt like 'doing a Jacky' on him and squatting on my behind to let out the biggest howl of frustration that I could muster. Gertie poked her head round the scullery door where she was frying some bacon in the frying pan on the stove.

'Bain't you goin, then?' she demanded.

'Yes we are!' and I was shouting at John, 'even if I have to go out to work to help pay for the damned thing.'

John's face was grim. 'You'll not do that,' he said. 'No wife of mine will go out to work. Your place is at home looking after my children and me.'

'Sounds just like a prison sentence,' I retorted sharply, 'which of course is precisely what it is.'

I decided that a king-sized sulk might bring quicker results and flounced upstairs. Alas, I was quickly coming to the realization that sulks, emotional blackmail or any other method had not the slightest effect upon my husband. Even a torrent of wrath pinged off the wall like spent bullets from a gun.

The following day I was staring miserably out of the window when I was surprised to hear John say,

'Get your coat on and we will go and have a look at this house. I am not promising anything, mind you, but there's no harm in having a look.'

So it happened that on a very grey and miserable day

162

with a fine misty drizzle falling, we all went to visit the house in Ullswater Road. The estate was vast and the streets were wide, and only on one side were the houses completed.

On the other side of the street, what was once a field was now a hive of activity. A giant bulldozer was busy gouging out chunks of earth in preparation for the foundations of yet another pair of houses. A concrete mixer kept up a steady whirr of grey mixture, and all along the green verge, piles of sand, cement, bricks and pantiles lay in neat little heaps. Sounds of hammering came from inside the half finished houses. As we made our way to the site manager's hut, we all stopped to look at this unfamiliar vista and to gaze at the huge high hoarding advertising the name of Laing.

The site manager took the keys to our house from a great row of them hanging along one side of the hut, and pointed across the muddy road to a completed block of four houses with an alleyway between. Most of the houses were semi-detached, and I experienced a tiny pang of disappointment. I would have preferred one of a pair. They seemed to me to be superior, a little less lumped together. Still, anything was better than the one room we were living in, and I quickly dismissed the feeling of dissatisfaction as unworthy, and followed John and the children over the rough boards that had been laid from the gate up to the front door. On this wet day, there seemed to be clods of yellow clay everywhere, but once inside the house, surveying the spacious rooms, and the cupboards, the greyness of the day was left behind, and I became excited and enthusiastic. John had brought a pad and pencil and was making small steps across the lounge in an attempt to estimate the amount of square yards of lino we would need. He did this several times and still wasn't very sure of his calculations at the end of it. I noted and admired the large bay window and asked him to measure the length for curtain material. This information also went into the book. Next came an inspection of the grate, which had a back boiler to give us hot water. It also had an iron shutter which, when pulled down, acted as a drawing device to raise the temperature and send the warmth through air vents let into the walls of all the other rooms. I thought this was an ingenious idea, but John scowled and said that this ingenious little gadget would probably eat up a ton of coal in no time flat. I remained silent after that, as my future depended on whether we could afford this brand new council house.

I wandered upstairs to view the bedrooms and to stand at the door to look around and imagine all of them carpeted and furnished in different colour schemes. When I came to the bathroom, this to me was the ultimate in luxury. Never in my whole life had I lived in a house with a bathroom. At South Road and at Repton Road, the tin bath was housed on the wall in the back yard and hung on a six inch nail, usually opposite the privy door, which was also outside. No more having to drag it down every week and boil up saucepans of hot water to have a bath. I closed my eyes in sheer ecstasy. Just thinking about it brought a feeling of pride at the thought of owning a bathroom. There was more. There was a toilet upstairs next to the bathroom and another in the garden along with a coalhouse and a shed. No more chamber pots under the bed and the drudgery of having to toil up and down the stairs with slop pails to empty the wretched things. I made my way down the stairs once more and into the kitchen. I opened drawers and cupboards, making little squeals of delight at the discovery of all the light and various up-to-date drawer space.

'Please God,' I prayed, 'let it be possible for us to move into this house,' and I vowed I would even go to work despite what my husband said about married women working.

When we had all gathered once more in the lounge, I waited for his verdict. He was still making notes in that pad of his, and his face had not relaxed at all. He

164

still wore the troubled look of a man about to start a life sentence. It wasn't at all the joyous occasion I had dreamed about. Two people, deliriously happy about the first home they were going to move into.

'Well,' he said at last, 'if your heart is set on it, I can just about manage it. Mind you,' and here his voice grew very firm and stern, 'I can only promise you the bread and not the butter. As it is, I shall have to do all the overtime on God's Earth to manage this little lot.'

'I'll get a job to help out,' I began, but he cut me short.

'Over my dead body,' he said, and the dark scowl returned to his face.

I knew we had not a stick of furniture of our own to bring with us, and I wondered at that moment how we would manage, but we held the key, and we were going to accept the house. The rest could take care of itself.

32 · *More Trials and Tribulations*

On a very cold day in February 1948, we finally moved into the house in Ullswater Road at Southmead. John had applied to the Soldiers Sailors and Airmen's Association for some money for furniture and removal expenses. They had generously given us thirty pounds and a voucher to obtain some surplus government blankets and beds. We bought twenty square yards of brown jasp lino, a very dingy solid brown floor covering used in offices and warehouses, which was going cheap because it was a discontinued line. It covered the lounge except for the bay. The damned stuff would not wear out and I grew sick of it long before it showed any sign of wear. A friend of John's who came out of the service at the same time was enterprising enough to start himself up in the upholstery business in the basement of his parents' house. His first attempt was a green hessian three piece suite which was not only big and ugly, but one of the chairs did not sit straight on account of the frame being warped and twisted. One night, when the two men had gone to the pub together, this great monstrosity was offered to John as a gift. An offer, John explained later, that he found it difficult to refuse. In fact, neither of us could find it easy to refuse such generosity, especially when he himself packed it in his van and delivered it to us the same day that we moved in, together with a bottle of British sherry to toast the success and good fortune of our new home. We sat in the bare bay window and drank out of cups. As yet, I had no wine glasses.

We strung up the curtains on wires. They were single sheets I had dyed a bright yellow, and looked very unprofessional up on wires that sagged dismally in the centre because we could not find the wire cutters. I never did get to like our unlovely green hessian suite, but I must give it full marks for the best play thing the girls ever had. The arms of the settee became horses that must have galloped half way round the globe, and the chairs, draped with an old sheet or blanket, made a wonderful tent. They printed the words 'Private, Keep Out' on a large piece of cardboard. From the giggles and contortions that went on inside that blanket, it was evident that a good time was being had by the pair of them.

One more item of furniture graced our lounge, taking pride of place in the far corner of the room next to the fireplace. Cash had been extracted from the thirty pounds that the Service Association allocated us for a writing bureau. John insisted that it was essential that he have one for all his private papers and kept it locked at all times. I protested that there should be no secrets between man and wife, but with a quiet stubbornness and air of superiority, the key was slipped on to his keyring and never once left his possession. I admit to having tried a few hundred keys in attempts to open it, but I was doomed to failure every time. The door always remained locked.

166

This, then, is the picture of our first lounge. There were no frills, such as pictures on the wall, or cushions for the chairs, but it was home, and everything else would come in time.

'Can't have everything at once,' was John's stoic comment; that and 'Rome wasn't built in a day.'

There were two wide doors painted a battleship grey to match the colour of everything else in the house, and these two doors divided the lounge from the small dinette. The frugal contents of this room comprised one full sized, white-topped table and four chairs. No sideboard graced the far wall, and a plain net curtain at the window did nothing to enhance the starkness or to encourage any of us to linger long over our meals. I scrubbed the table top the way of the grain religiously every week, and polished the black bitumen floor to a high degree of brilliance with lavender polish.

The girls had two hospital iron beds and there was an abundance of army surplus blankets. Two lockers and single wardrobes graced their rooms. They had been quite generous to us at the stores, and when we had more cash, we meant to go again. I had very recklessly gone into debt over our bedroom and bought a Utility full sized bed and dressing table. I chose a warm shade of mahogany, and well remember the telling off I received from John, who thought I was far too extravagant for going twenty pounds into debt.

There was one other extravagance which nobody grumbled about and was enjoyed by all in that bitter February of '48. I had the foresight to order a whole ton of coal, and paid the coal man two quid plus a tip when he delivered it into our brand new coal house. I counted the bags as he passed by the window and along the alleyway. I was thinking how wonderful it was that he was not coming through the hall. I had deliberately kept back some of the money we had been given, for this purpose. The back boiler gave us lashings of hot water, and the warm air vents kept the chill off the dinette. Best of all, the boards in the bedrooms were always warm to walk on. Cold lino and freezing rooms became a bad dream of the past. However, just as John predicted, the fire gobbled up the coal. If you wanted a warm house, it demanded to be fed. Sometimes the coal man came, dropped in a couple of bags of coal, and because I was stony broke, I pretended I wasn't in. The coal bill grew alarmingly, but still I couldn't pay. Although I knew that the day of reckoning would come, and I would have to face the wrath of my spouse, what was waiting for me remained mercifully concealed.

John found out about the coal bill when someone from the coal merchant called to ask about the unpaid bill. John said he knew nothing about any unpaid bill, and the caller was invited in to the house for an explanation. He was a middle-aged man, and was obviously very aware of the explosive situation he had created. His tone was apologetic and conciliatory. He explained that his firm would accept two shillings off the arrears per week and still continue to deliver two hundredweight of coal. They did not want to be responsible for any hardship in a cold spell. He made out a debit card for the amount due and very leniently said he would accept five shillings off the arrears. Silent and white faced, John handed over the five bob and courteously showed the man to the door. When he returned to the room, he just as quietly told me that I was no longer to be trusted with money, and from now on, the rent and other bills would be paid by him and all the cash I would ever handle would be for housekeeping. I was not only extravagant, I was secretive too. Well, it was evident that the small amount of house-keeping he left me was far from adequate, but when I protested, he pulled out the linings of his pockets to prove to me that he couldn't give what he didn't have. It was clear that I would have to find a part time job.

Next door was a four bedroomed house occupied by a family of six lads whose ages ranged from eighteen down to a boy of six. We never did see any sign of a father, but their mother was well in evidence. She was a big, blousy woman who ruled the roost and kept the boys in order and her word was law. They played football in the alley-way and drove me crazy. When the ball was kicked onto the garden, they trampled all over it and the gate was continually left open when, without so much as a by-your-leave, they walked in to retrieve their ball. No amount of yelling had the slightest effect, they merely scooped up the ball and, with cheeky grins, kicked it down the alley. I swore I would confiscate the damn thing the very next time they kicked it over to my garden. Finally, in desperation, I retrieved the ball and carried it triumphantly into the house.

Round came Mrs Cook a few seconds later, and with arms akimbo demanded the return of the ball.

'The kids have to play somewhere,' she said belligerently. 'Your ol' man wants to give you a couple of lads, then you might be more tolerant towards 'em.'

'I believe in quality, not quantity,' I said icily, and almost shoved the ball in her face. Matters were not improved when, every time John came home and they were still playing in the alley, he actually joined in the game with them. Obviously, this made John a 'rattling good bloke' and me a 'miserable old bag'.

Meanwhile, at every opportunity, Jacky would slip out the back way and through the alley to cross the road to the site manager's hut. Here she was spoilt with cups of tea and biscuits and cakes. I saw the danger behind every pile of sand and bricks but, despite all my scolding, that was where Miss Jacky could always be found.

When Pat arrived home from school one afternoon, it was already getting dark. I called for her to go and collect Jacky and come for tea. Half an hour later, Pat returned on her own, Jacky was nowhere to be found, and the Site Manager had not seen her since three o'clock. I experienced a ring of fear. Telling Patty to have her tea and remain in the house until I returned, I ran over the road to survey the area. The piles of bricks and pantiles

Auntie Gwen holding Jacky, around 1946

seemed dark and alien in the gloom now that there was
no sign of activity to give them life or meaning. When I
called her name, the brooding silence seemed to mock:
  'She is not here, she is not here.'
Where could I begin to look for her? Perhaps she was

in some other child's house, I could try knocking on doors. I looked up the deserted street with dismay. 'Please God, show me where she is,' I prayed, then began to laugh hysterically. Why do we call on an unseen force as a last resort? I shivered and realised that I had come out without a coat. I would need a torch. How stupid of me to come without a torch. I suddenly thought of the pond at the edge of the estate. I closed my eyes. Jacky would not venture that far, she had been warned never to go that far. I tried not to think of the pond.

When I got back to the house, Mrs Cook was leaning over the gate. As I approached, she spoke to me with real concern in her voice.

'Our Charlie's round your house with your bigger girl, she come crying round our house saying she was frit, and that your little 'un's lost. I've sent our Sidney out on his bike to have a scout round the block. If I was you, I'd let my eldest come round with you to have a look through they half finished houses up top there. Kids da sometimes like playing there.'

I looked at her, not comprehending. When long evening shadows fell, what child would dream of lingering? Darkness sent children home to warm fires and security. However, her concern did make me feel less cut off and helpless. There was another person with me now and I was able to breathe more easily. She broke off to shout for Frank, her eldest boy. Her voice was strident and authoritative. Frank was suddenly by her side.

'Go with Missus and search they houses up top. If they'm locked, get our Sidney to ride to the Site Manager's house along there in Southmead road, he da know where he lives.'

Frank was already loping over the rough uneven ground. He was a tall angular fellow and seemed all arms and legs. Mrs Cook called after us, 'Have 'ee got the torch, Frank?'

He waved it aloft for her to see, and as I ran by his side she was still calling after us,

171

'Don't 'ee worry about your big girl, we'll have her in wi' we.'

All the houses on the other side of the street were empty and locked. We made our way round to the backs of them and tried shining the torch through the windows, but it was impossible to see or even pierce the blackness within. I fell over an empty five gallon paint tin, dislodging it so that it rolled over, making a clatter that started a dog barking somewhere further down the street. I lay there on the damp earth. I wasn't hurt but prayed that I might hear another sound above all those noises of the night. I almost sobbed with relief when I heard Sidney arrive. He jumped off his bike and leaned it against the side of the house. He jangled the keys in front of me and helped me to my feet. All three of us went systematically through the houses shining the torch and calling for Jacky. There was one last house to search, and as the key was inserted in the lock, I was the first through the door and into the kitchen. The torch circled the room and picked out the form of a small child crouched in a corner but not saying a word. Her eyes were wide with terror so that I rushed forward and held her in my arms. She shivered with cold and shock, and I tried not to think of the hours that she had been there, or how scared she must have been when the foreman had locked the door, unaware that she had been playing there. Frank took off his coat for me to wrap her trembling little body. Every so often, little dry sobs shook her small frame.

'I called you Mummy,' she said at last, 'I called you and you didn't come.'

l was crying with her now, and the two lads turned away. 'I'll always be here when you call, Jacky,' I said and held her closer.

'l must have heard you, because here I am.' The two lads helped me to my feet and together we walked back down the street. Mrs Cook gave a grunt of satisfaction and disappeared with the two boys inside the house.

172

Frank brought Patty round ten minutes later. I gave Jacky a hot drink and put her to bed.

Several days later, the lads were playing football in the alley again, and the ball was once more kicked on to the garden. I gave a sigh and waited for the sound of boots outside the window. To my surprise, there was a knock on the front door instead. When I opened the door, Charlie stood there, smiling timidly.

'Please Missus, I'm sorry about this but the ball's gone on your garden, do you mind if I get it please?'

I was so taken aback that I stared at him until he began to shuffle uncomfortably. Then I laughed and blurted out, 'Of course you can.'

I suddenly felt that I was making progress.

33 · The Alarm Clock

The houses were completed and the pavements laid. The site manager's hut was dismantled and the board with Laing's name printed on it long gone. Trees began to appear in the front gardens and at weekends, men could be seen digging energetically, preparing the uncultivated soil for fruit and vegetables and flowers. Across the road a Doctor's Surgery opened up and much to everybody's surprise, a woman doctor attended there. A storm of protest greeted the new arrival. Comments at the local newsagent and post office ranged from 'Fancy! We've got a lady doctor in Dunmail Road' to 'Tain't right [this from the men] having to drop yer trousers in front of a woman.'

Despite all the prejudice, she stayed, along with all the other changes going on around us.

The Welfare State ushered in a new world for all the poor, but especially for women. For the first time, women visited the doctor on their own account. Before, it was all they could do to get the kids there in emergencies, and it was common to see women almost limping with the pain of ulcers, bad veins, and worse. Minor ailments would drag on and on, dosed up with home remedies or ineffective preparations like Beechams Powders or Doan's Little Liver Pills. (Beecham's Pills, taken in great quantities, were also used to try and end unwanted pregnancies, but of course, never worked.) Free hospital and dental treatment, and the Family Allowance for the second child delighted us, although the latter brought such a storm of protest from the men because they thought their own wages might be affected as a consequence. John threatened to cut my housekeeping by eight shillings but he reckoned without my aggression, which was pretty frightening when I got angry. When danger threatened, I went out to meet it. Like a duellist with rapier drawn, my first move was to cross swords and deliver the cry of 'on guard!' My spouse was no coward, but he saw the sense in surrender.

'You dock my money,' I said, 'and I will feed the kids but not you. I still have the housekeeping to take charge of.'

A few weeks later, Woolworths were advertising for counterhands and Mrs Cook offered to look after Jacky so that l could earn a few extra quid a week. It was only a part-time job, just a few minutes walk away, and I was home again by two o'clock. I was working for a whole week before John found out. Reprisal came swift and sure, and the first week's wages was stopped from my housekeeping.

'Now that you have your own money, you don't need mine,' was his caustic remark.

'If you don't pay me,' I said with equal determination, 'I withdraw my services and you buy and get your own food.'

John was not an aggressive man. He merely held this weird idea that the little woman must stay at home to be protected. It must have worried him to discover that he

174

had married a woman with such strong views. One that he could not subdue bothered him still further. He capitulated after a week. I had the housekeeping, plus a few quid of my own. The very first thing I bought for the house was some new curtains with rufflette tape and curtain rail that allowed the curtain rings to slide easily along the curtain track. How proud I was when I stood back to look at them and to swish them from side to side.

Things were not so well with John. He hated the early morning shifts and the late night ones. Most of all he hated the job. Being a conductor on the buses was not his vocation. In the morning, he yawned incessantly and his blue eyes were red and bloodshot through lack of sleep. He worked long hours and when he finally staggered through the door, he was half asleep in the chair before it was even time for bed. I urged him to ease up on the overtime, now things were a bit easier. He was tired and irritable and that was not much help to me.

In order to help him to get up in the mornings, John had an alarm with a big double bell which he put in the cover of a biscuit tin by the side of the bed. When it went off in the early hours, it danced around in the tin and almost made me jump out of my skin. John would still be fast asleep, snoring away, whilst everybody else would be wide awake. Jacky would demand tea and bikkies, and make her way to the stairs. There'd be nothing for it but to start the day before the dawn had a chance to break through. I swore vengeance, and threatened I would throw the clock out of the window, if this state of affairs carried on for much longer.

Tempers were short and tension mounting. As we prepared for bed, I saw John stubbornly winding up the alarm. Why the hell did he bother, if he never heard it when it did go off, I fumed. The clock was placed reverently square in the middle of the tin, and with a couple of grunts, John settled down and was soon fast in dreamland. When he lay on his back, he always ground his teeth, a habit which set my own teeth on edge for

175

every grind was like a knife scraping on a plate. I prodded him in the back until he half opened his eyes to enquire stupidly, 'Wha', wha', what?' then roll over on to his side taking half the bedclothes with him. I sighed and tried in vain to retrieve a corner of the eiderdown. Oh, for a single bed and my own room, I thought viciously.

I eventually drifted off to sleep, and dreamed I was flying over emerald green grass. I had a heightened sensation of colours in strange lines that I could not name. Around me flew glorious birds of paradise which moved like animated clockwork toys. When I came to the sea, I experienced a sense of excitement, for this wide expanse of water was the beginning of a great adventure. Just at that moment, a warning seemed to sound in my head, almost like a command to stop flying and come down to terra firma once more. I was being urged to return at once to my body before the bell sounded. I turned to run but found I could not move. I strained with all my might to move my limbs. Then this awful bell sounded in my brain and I woke with such a fright that I thought my heart had jumped right out of my body. With my ticker thumping like mad, and feeling so angry I could have screamed, I picked up the offending alarm clock now dancing around in the tin and emitting this deafening and raucous ringing. I carried it to the top of the stairs and threw it with great force, right to the bottom, where it bounced on the three bottom steps then crashed onto the black bitumen floor of the darkened hall. The glass broke into tiny fragments scattering everywhere, together with all the tiny parts of its innards. Finally the main spring flew dejectedly out with a mournful 'dong' and then there was silence.

I went back to collect Jacky, who was by now repeating 'tea, bikkies, tea, bikkies' and strode downstairs with her to put her none too gently into her chair and to put the kettle on for an early cup of tea. Patty followed, quietly and cautiously. She had a fine nose for atmosphere and could tell I was distraught. We drank our tea in silence.

176

Both girls now sensed the drama, and I was not going to budge in my determination not to rouse my spouse for work. The fraught situation demanded that he saw for himself that the alarm system was not going to work. A drastic situation called for drastic measures.

Some hours later, I returned from seeing Patty to school and was coming in through the front door. The clock was still strewn all over the floor. I had no intention of removing it. I glanced up the stairs where a slight movement arrested my attention. John was on the top stair, looking very comical dressed only in his little short vest and striped briefs. He was bleary-eyed and yawning, and scratching himself. He was still trying to shake off sleep and to focus on the consciousness of day. Between yawns, he was endeavouring to ask 'Wos the time?' His first shock came when I calmly told him it was nine o'clock. The second came when he blinked and finally saw the clock and its contents scattered across the floor. The effect was electrifying and he began to jump up and down on the top stair, rather like Rumplestiltskin.

'You've broken my clock, you've broken my clock,' he kept repeating, as though he couldn't believe I would ever dare to do such a thing even though I had threatened to so many times. Without another word, he dressed and went out. Not even a cup of tea did he make or ask for. His face was as expressionless as the times he played cards with the boys. I knew a reprisal raid would come, but not when. There was a dark side to my husband. I could seemingly win, but not for long.

Friday came, and conversation had flagged between us somewhat. My Lord and Master was not pleased with me and that was evident. Every time he came through the door, I could tell by the expression on his face that the time for forgiving was not yet, and I must suffer some more. However, I noticed that he was carrying a small square parcel under his arm, which he placed carefully and lovingly in the centre of the table.

'Ahh,' I thought impulsively, 'today is the day when all

177

is forgiven, he has brought me a present.' I managed a smile to show that I was all in favour of this arrangement and he placed the wrapped parcel in my hands. Inside, I heard the unmistakable ticking of a time bomb clock. The smile froze on my face. I knew exactly what that parcel contained and I wasn't wrong. A replica of the clock that had bounced down the stairs even to the same colour.

'Try aiming that one down the stairs,' said my spouse, in cold unemotional tones, and he placed my housekeeping allowance by the side of the mocking ticking clock. When I picked it up to check it, it was exactly thirty shillings short. That was the amount that the clock had cost.

34 · *Christmas Dinner*

There were precious Sundays when John did not have to work. On these days we would take the children for long walks, or sometimes a bus ride to Blaise Castle and the Hamlet, which was a favourite of Pat's. Eastville Park was another, then through to Channons Hill and Snuff Mills, where I could relive all the memories of my own childhood through the joy of my children. Long before the motorway was introduced along the bottom of Muller Road, there used to be a row of exciting shops on the right hand side opposite to one of the entrances to the park. You had to walk up some steps to the small promenade in front of the shops. Outside was an assortment of the most exciting things, such as black and white plimsols which we called daps, coloured buckets and spades, beach balls, and, finally, bundles of fishing nets. Most children bought one of these, and a small army of them wended their way to the river that flowed so boisterously by the side of the wooden bridge at Snuff Mills.

Glass jam jars held by string tied around the lip were a common feature. Even the girls demanded one when they knew we were bound for that magic place. The bags of bread rolls and the lemonade were also a 'must', plus a stop at this certain shop on the way.

John was very good with the two girls and played with them for hours. He even tucked up his own trousers and went with them into the water to help them catch the tiddlers as they darted from under the rocks in great shoals. I took this golden opportunity to slip away on my own. It was heavenly walking through the woods, smelling the odour of the damp leaves and looking up through the gently swaying leaves of the trees. I needed the room and the time to be on my own, to let the peace and the quiet seep into my very soul. John would sense my absence almost the second that I had gone. He never, ever, understood my need for it. He'd always come looking for me after about twenty minutes, with the excuse that he was worried about me and that anything might happen. I got the impression by the scowl on his face that, as I was his possession, it was his right to protect me from hidden dangers that only he was aware of and of which I had no knowledge. It was true that his intrusion into my sacred privacy tended to irritate and annoy me, although I could not have explained why this should be so at the time. That bold open stare that accompanied the end of the search for me conveyed triumph for him, but inevitability for me. I wrestled with these feelings, knowing they were there, but not understanding them.

This feeling that I had done something beyond the bounds would persist for the rest of the day, so that it seemed that I must exert myself to do extra things for my spouse in order to appease him. If I wanted the atmosphere to be lightness and brightness again, I would have to work extra hard to maintain it. Alas, as I was always at a loss as to the complex nature of my husband's mind, the spark that set the explosion alight was never

179

far away. Preferring the direct approach, I would usually demand after a reasonable period of suffering —

'What the hell is the matter with you?'

On one occasion, his answer struck a kind of paranoid fear in my heart that almost paralysed me.

'I would like another child. A son.'

Ever since that sad little miscarriage, not another word had been mentioned, but it had left a scar on my memory and I was now afraid of sex and its consequences. Because of the doctor's attitude, I was afraid to go for advice and, at that time, few people knew about family planning clinics. This startling request, delivered as a cold and stern demand, brought a violent reaction from me.

'So you want the Queen Bee act again from me. You can't keep the family you already have, and here you are insisting on another.'

'You refuse, then?' His voice remained cool and infuriating.

'Yes.'

'You know that your refusal could mean that I could divorce you?'

I suddenly wanted to cry. I wanted the comfort and the cuddles. Somehow, I knew that tears would be an act of submission that would be the only thing my husband would be satisfied with. Don't let me feel anything, my brain whispered. Neither love nor hate.

'Do your worst and be damned to you,' I said, and went downstairs to lie on our coarse hessian sofa.

I lost the job at Woolworths a month before our first Christmas at Ullswater Road. Jacky developed chicken pox and demanded attention. Day and night, I sat with her, painting her spots and trying to prevent her from scratching the itchy patches on her skin. It was a bit of a blow, because those few extra pounds would have made all the difference that first festive season in buying modest little gifts for the girls. However, I was well aware that my child's health came first, and consoled myself with the thought that, come what may, we would make

180

the best of what we had, and commenced to buy small stocking fillers for the girls to open on Christmas Day. At least the kids were kept happy, and I kept them busy gluing together packets of paper chains that I had brought from the store before I had to leave. The paper chains were strung from the four corners of the room and caught up in the centre just above the light by a big paper bell. We even had a small tree. Silver tinsel hung from the branches, and we made tiny silver points on the tips of the branches by covering them with silver foil. The fairy on the topmost branch was cut out in cardboard and strips of tinsel were glued on to cover her wings and to make a skirt for her dress. Patty came up with an ingenious idea and made paper lanterns that she finally crayoned and then hung round the room. They spent hours pasting and cutting out pictures to make their own calendars and Christmas cards. In the makeshift tent, they were silent but busy little bees, spending hours cutting and snipping at mysterious presents for their friends and for us.

'Promise you won't look,' they would plead, and the big cardboard notice with 'Private Keep Out' was well displayed.

We had four unexpected visitors that Christmas. Strange to say, if it had not been for the arrival of these four people and the goodies that they brought, our Christmas would have been very lean indeed.

We had been awakened early on Christmas morning by the cautious creeping about of the two girls who, having discovered their coloured stockings at the bottom of the bed, were tearing at the gift wrapped packages inside. The brand new crayons and book and the cut out dolls would keep them quiet for the rest of the morning and allow me. to get on with the dinner. John would be away down the pub. I had already laid down the law that I did not want to wait too long for dinner and wanted him home on the dot. However, if our first Christmas dinner was a test piece, it set a pattern that was to be repeated throughout our marriage. He did not return until two-thirty. He then disappeared to sleep it off and dinner was a sad and pathetic attempt at making do without dear Daddy. He emerged bleary-eyed and yawning round about tea time.

I had washed the pots and savagely covered the uneaten lunch and slammed it in the oven, where I vowed it would remain until it was needed, and he could do the honours on that one. With a final last flick of the dishcloth round the sink, I glanced up in surprise when there came a loud rat-a-tat-tat at the front door, and both girls ran to open it and admit Dennis and Audrey, and my mother and father. They came bearing gifts for all of us, together with wine, Christmas cake and pudding, both home-made by my mother, and a large trifle which Audrey declared was liberally splashed with sherry, with real cream on the top.

I was so surprised that I couldn't say a word. Den put the presents round the tree, and Audrey tied gold covered chocolate coins and crackers on the tree. I loved Audrey from the moment I saw her. She began to tell me about the council house that she had been allocated at Fortfield Road and how excited she was.

'You should see our Den's place,' cut in my Mother, 'it's lovely, not like this barn of a place.'

Dad went out to inspect the garden we hadn't touched. He was quite right to think it a wilderness: John had not been exaggerating when he stated that a window box was about his limit. John heard the commotion and put in an appearance. He even woke up enough to allow himself to be dressed up in an old red dressing gown and a copious beard made from a wad of cotton wool. All this was done very secretly out in the hallway with Audrey urging the girls to be very quiet and they would hear Santa arriving on his sleigh. Presently, we heard the sound of the sleigh bells ringing, and we all began to sing Jingle Bells. The girls' eyes were as big and as round as saucers, and they sat as quiet as mice when this big man

182

in red advanced to the small tree and began to distribute presents all round. My mother had given them baby dolls which she had dressed herself. I had a huge parcel. When the wrappings had been hastily torn away, I found inside a pair of green plaster of Paris water carriers. I enthused and twittered with joy about these delicate little forms and promptly gave them a place of honour in the window bay. Alas, they were not fated to stay there long, because one very wet day about six weeks later, the girls, bored with not being able to go out, began to play catchers in the lounge. The ball knocked one of the plaster images right over and it smashed to smithereens on the bitumen floor. Whilst the two girls stood there in petrified fear and trepidation at what they had done, I removed the potential for another unpredicted accident by swiping its twin on to the floor and breaking that one as well. Both girls sobbed loud and long until I also sobbed loud and long with them, me for the loss of my beloved plaster water carriers and to assure the girls that I forgave them and would they forgive me too.

However, that Christmas day was as near to perfection as I could ever wish for. Den had brought bottles of port and sherry to drink our health and to the success of both our houses, and mince pies and sausage rolls that Audrey had made which proved her to be a wonderful cook.

'I say, Joy,' she repeated over and over, 'your Den's lovely. I can't wait to get him home in bed.'

Den laughed good-naturedly and replied, 'Joyce, she's like an octopus. All arms and legs.'

It was a wonderful day. I was sorry when they all trooped through the hall and bundled into Dad's little car and drove off. Mum and Dad were staying at Audrey's in their new house at Hengrove. They were now running a cafe at Bruton, and I had been given an invitation to come and spend a holiday there as soon as the weather was nice enough. Dad said we were to let him know and he would come and fetch us all in the car. After they were gone, I had this warm feeling that things were getting better. I had made a friend of my sister-in-law, who insisted that we keep in touch with each other, and Mum and Dad had helped to make that day so special.

When you come to the end of a perfect day
And you sit alone with your thoughts —
The bells ring out in a carol gay
For the joy that the day has brought.

I began to hum the tune of this song. I was happy that day.

35 · *The Prefab*

The early months of 1950 were extremely cold. Both girls were going to school now, and four times a day I would have to take and fetch them, carrying macs if it was raining, making sure that I was there outside the school to escort them over the busy road. Sometimes, I visited the Co-op to get something for tea. The girls loved to come with me and would stand spellbound watching the cash for the goods stuffed into little wood screw-topped containers and sent spinning along overhead wires into the cash desk in the middle of the hall. Along with the change, there would also be checks given for the amount of money spent. At the end of the year, a cash dividend would be exchanged for all the money you had spent with the Co-op during that time. This came in handy, especially at Christmas. I became a member of the Co-op very early in my married life.

The actual checks were marvellous make-pretend money to play post offices and shops with. The girls played happily with the Co-op checks for hours.

Now that we had free dental treatment for the children, we were informed that a visit to the clinic at Southmead was essential, and regular visits became almost routine. The child was handed a paper requesting that we attend on a certain day. That morning, I looked out at the weather and wished that my journey was not necessary. It was bitterly cold and it was a fair step to the clinic, which was half way up the hill.

The hall was packed with parents and schoolchildren, all sitting on benches. The school dentist did not carry very good memories for me. I remembered in my far off school days, our clinic had been at Verrier Road at Redfield and a long tram ride almost into town. All the kids filed in the hall to wait outside the dentist's room. When it was your turn to go in, you were told to open your mouth wide and not to be a baby and start to cry. They then whipped out teeth willy-nilly, shoved a big wad of cotton wool into your mouth and showed you the door. I remember some of the parents indignantly shouting out that they were nothing else but bloody butchers, and escorting their tearful offspring away as quickly as possible.

I hoped my own child would not be put to this particular form of torture. In fact, I prayed that the interview would be nothing more than a quick check up with no fillings or extractions necessary. Sometimes, when a tooth needed to be extracted, the kids had gas and air administered in the form of a balloon which they were asked to blow up. I shuddered when I thought of gas and air. I remembered unpleasant experiences connected with this primitive method. I began to wish that John could have had the distasteful task of bringing Patty here to this somewhat uncivilised gathering. Lots of the children were already scared and beginning to cry before they were even called. Apprehension and fear travelled round the room quickly. I assured Patty that I would not allow them to take any of her teeth out unless she herself agreed that they should. She looked at me, not really believing me, until I held both her hands and convinced her that I was not only listening to her, but that I was completely in earnest and in sympathy with her wishes. We both felt relieved and more settled after that.

185

Pat then began to talk to a small child of about five or six who was sitting next to her. An older woman who was obviously her grandmother or perhaps an elderly aunt, was fussing round her and trying to stop her from fidgeting and sliding all over the seat. Her story was soon tumbling out. It needed only a sympathetic listener. She was the child's grandmother, as we surmised, and she had come all the way from Leicester to look after Trudy, because her daughter had died very tragically of cancer. She wished the prefab was bigger, it only had two bed-rooms and she had to share a bedroom with Trudy. If it were possible to get a bigger house, on an exchange basis, she would gladly sell up and come down to Bristol to look after her son-in-law and his little daughter.

I sat staring at her, not comprehending at first, or able to find the right words. I was tongue-tied. I knew this was a heaven sent opportunity for me to get my prefab, but this chance was so startlingly sharp and direct, coming like a bolt out of the blue, it made me stutter for words. I heard the nurse calling Patty's name and stumbled over the words that, in their turn, made her look at me with incredulity.

'I've got a house I can't afford. I should love a prefab. I've always wanted one. Look out for me when we have finished with the dentist, and I'll give you my address. Won't do any harm to come down to have a look will it?'

She nodded in assent and I moved away holding on to Pat's hand, determined that I would demand that I go into that dreaded room with her and to stand by what I had promised her.

At the door, a tall thin-lipped nurse tried to disen-tangle the hold on our hands, derisively saying to Pat,

'You are a big girl now, you don't need your mother with you, do you?'

'I need to be with her,' I cut in determinedly, 'I need to know the results of the examination.'

Very reluctantly, she allowed me to go in and a very big male dentist with a shock of red hair and a white dental gown drew up a chair for me to sit on. He began immediately, with the aid of a female nurse, to check Patty's teeth, calling out in numbers as he checked them. When he had finished, he addressed me curtly.

'Your daughter has two slightly tipped teeth, that will need to be extracted. If you will kindly leave the room now, we can get on with the job.'

John had often told me of the wonderful job they did in filling and saving the teeth of servicemen. A tooth was only extracted as a very last resort.

'Can the teeth not be filled?' I enquired, and watched a shade of impatience settle on his face. Patty sat looking at the both of us. I fought her cause that day.

Finally he gave up the fight. It was obvious that he now wanted to be rid of us as quickly as possible.

'Make an appointment for a further visit,' he said testily, 'I will see what can be done.'

Patty was up out of the chair and holding my hand again. In the corridor we spied Trudy and her Gran awaiting her turn. I sat down by the side of them and began writing out my address and handing it to her. I explained the way and how she would best get there. Trudy was screwing her handkerchief, I could see she was a bundle of nerves. I could also see that all her teeth in the front were black. No amount of bullying on Gran's part would save them. I smiled at Trudy, then looked at Gran.

'Hope to see you soon, then,' and waved them both goodbye.

When we got outside the gate, I looked at Pat and grinned. 'Chase you down the hill,' I said.

About a week later, she kept her word and came to see me. She was delighted with the house and said she would bring her son to see it and to meet my husband.

'Although,' she admitted laughingly, 'he won't mind where he lives as long as I am satisfied.'

John did not put up any resistance. The prefab would be much cheaper to run and relieve the worry of the

Jacky, Joyce and Pat outside the prefab

endless bills and trying to maintain the upkeep of the larger house. We were invited back to the prefab in St Lucia Crescent and saw the warmth and the comfort that this small dwelling could give. I had so much to thank these two people for. They left the carpets and the curtains.

'They might as well stay,' I was told, 'they will never fit in your house.'

Gran had enough furniture to fill the house at Ullswater Road, so the three piece suite was left as well and so was a red-topped bakelite table that fitted the alcove in the kitchen. Both men went to the Council House to ask permission to exchange, and on a very sunny day in April 1950, we moved into the prefab.

When the van which had conveyed all our pathetic little bits and pieces to our new address had moved away, I watched John putting up the children's beds in the sunny room facing the lawn. Sounds of their happy laughter came to me through the open window. John came to stand beside me and together we watched the two girls playing happily together. The prefab was my dream come true. The image of a cottage with roses round the door had kept the dream alive all through those weary war years. A home and children was the happy ending to all the books and films we had ever read or seen. Why was it, then, that on that sunny April day, with the birds singing, and the little house calling, a tiny doubt like a dark cloud on the horizon kept nagging at me?

'You will be happy here?'

John's voice cut across the silence. It seemed that in the question lay the answer.

As if in a dream, I saw myself once again walking down the aisle, and heard the loud slamming of the door. From the moment little girls are given cold china dolls to play with, to nurse and to care for, this is their destiny and ultimate ending. There is nothing else outside the narrow creativity of a home and family. I saw myself like a floating piece of seaweed half submerged. Against the quickened thumping of my heartbeat, and the desire to escape, I saw my mother's eyes burn into mine.

'Don't think your life will be any different to mine.'

The words — the awful inevitability. It seemed that from somewhere outside a cold wind blew.

189